A Year across Maryland

A YEAR ACROSS

MARYLAND

· *A Week-by-Week Guide* ·
to Discovering Nature in the Chesapeake Region

BRYAN MACKAY

The Johns Hopkins University Press
Baltimore

This book has been brought to publication with the generous assistance of the Chesapeake Audubon Society.

The Johns Hopkins University Press
2715 North Charles Street
Baltimore, Maryland 21218-4363
www.press.jhu.edu

Photographs are by the author except for those on the following pages: Scott Bauer, USDA, 203; Lavon Kara Brown, 90; William J. Hubick, 22, 53, 59, 138, 226, 258; Frode Jacobsen, 7, 13, 57, 68, 80, 101, 113, 133, 145, 153, 196, 208, 269; Debra MacKay, 66, 75, 79, 184, 225; Pamela C. Platt, 35; Hugh Simmons, 55, 64, 179, 282.

The Library of Congress Cataloging-in-Publication Data for this book will be found on the last printed page of the book.

Special discounts are available for bulk purchases of this book. For more information, please contact Special Sales at 410-516-6936 or specialsales@press.jhu.edu.

The Johns Hopkins University Press uses environmentally friendly book materials, including recycled text paper that is composed of at least 30 percent post-consumer waste, whenever possible.

Contents

MARCH

APRIL

MAY

JUNE

JULY

AUGUST

September

October

November

December

Acknowledgments

I've been interested in nature ever since my ecology field trips with Professor Bob Platt during college. That has now been about forty years ago. Almost a decade after college, time afield with Dr. Charley Stine introduced me to some of Maryland's superb natural landscapes and habitats, many of which I revisit often and with great pleasure. And during one growing season, about 1974, I botanized with Bill Brown, the old herb man of Oella; he told wonderful stories about plants that, even if only folklore, were always engaging. More recently, I am especially indebted to the many contributors to Maryland Osprey and its successor, mdbirding, listservs chronicling observations of birds in our state; their contributors are an especially active, informative, helpful, and courteous group of naturalists.

Many other individuals provided observations or insights to me personally for this book. They include Hugh Simmons, Ruth Bergstrom, Phil Pannill, Theaux Le Gardeur, Rodger Waldman, Nick Caloyianis, Martin Gary, Tim Smith, Cynthia O'Rourke, Dave Curson, Esther Fleischman, Pamela Platt, Les Roslund, Sue Ricciardi, Mark Scallion, Frode Jacobsen, Kathy Woods, and Debi MacKay.

I am indebted to the many friends and acquaintances who have accompanied me during more than thirty years of exploring Maryland and adjacent states on paddling trips, hikes, photographic excursions, birding trips, bike rides, and just plain messing around in nature looking to see what's there. The list is too long, and my memory too faulty, to list everyone, but know that I have valued your companionship and benefited from your enthusiasm and camaraderie.

Several skilled photographers have very generously contributed images to this book, and to them I am immensely grateful. They include Frode Jacobsen, Bill Hubick, Debi MacKay, Hugh

Simmons, Lavon Kara Brown, and Pamela Platt. These photos greatly enrich this book, and I appreciate the artistic vision of these photographers.

The "Notes from the Field" for September first appeared, in a slightly different version, in *Canoe and Kayak* in August 1999, and I am grateful to the magazine for permission to reprint it here.

A gift from Chesapeake Audubon Society to the Johns Hopkins University Press has helped bring this book to publication. I am immensely thankful to my colleagues on the board of directors of Chesapeake Audubon for this assistance.

This is my third book published by the Johns Hopkins University Press, and I am thankful for the Press's willingness to believe in me and these projects. Bob Brugger and Jack Holmes have been especially encouraging, and I appreciate their support over the past twenty years. My editor for this book, Greg Nicholl, has been wonderfully supportive and has provided important advice and insight that has improved *A Year across Maryland*. Anne Whitmore copy edited this book, and I value her professional expertise.

Finally, I give special thanks to my wife, Debi MacKay, who has enthusiastically ventured into the field with me for the last nine years, enduring hunger, thirst, fatigue, sunburn, poison ivy, mosquitoes, and chiggers, all without complaint and always with a smile. She is simply the best.

Introduction

To every thing there is a season, and a time to every
purpose under the heaven.

Eccles. 3:1

King Solomon, the reputed author of the book of Ecclesiastes,
got it right: there *is* a time under heaven, not just for every human
purpose but for every natural phenomenon as well. The cycle
of seasons rolls on, and those of us who love the ever-changing
events of the year can barely wait for the next act in nature's play.
Will spring be late arriving this year? Can we find our favorite
wildflower in the same location, in the same abundance, as in
the past? Will autumn storms bring interesting vagrant birds to
our shores? What experiences await us in our time afield; what
memories will we make, alone and with friends and family, as
we travel among the living things that inhabit our world? The
seasons are a paradox: natural events are predictable and follow a
regular pattern, yet variations are inevitable and seem capricious.
Like performances of a work of good music, the notes are always
the same, but how they are played is never identical.

 This book is a chronicle of some of the more familiar and
best-loved periodic natural events here in Maryland and just
beyond the borders of our Free State. The great majority of the
descriptions in this book stem from my personal experiences in
the field. I kept formal field notes in 2010 and 2011, once I had
formed the idea for this book. In addition, there are some idio-
syncratic observances—arrivals and departures that have caught
my attention over the years. Certainly some of your favorite
changes in the natural world may be missing. For this I beg your
forgiveness. The list is by necessity just a sampling. Neither the
blooming time of every wildflower nor the arrival date of every
migratory bird is included; other books and websites should

be consulted for this level of detail, and some of my favorites among these resources are listed in the bibliography at the end of this book.

Attentive observers of nature will realize that the placement of natural events within a specific week is only an approximation. I have tried to assign a particular event to the week when you are *most likely* to be able to see it occur. Hence, you may well find a certain wildflower blooming in advance of the week indicated, but the date in this book is when you will have the greatest chance of encountering that species in flower. Of course these dates may vary from year to year, depending on weather, and even climate; global warming is happening, and it is already changing the phenology of our natural world. Likewise, where you are in Maryland affects periodic biological phenomena, more so for plants than for birds. Winter lingers late and arrives early on Maryland's Appalachian Plateau in far western Garrett County, while the same is true for autumn on the wetlands of the Eastern Shore. Driving Interstate 95 during the third week in April gives a sense of the remarkable degree to which even small changes in latitude affect leaf formation in trees.

There are forty-eight chapters in this book, four for each month of the year (the calendar distributes the remaining four weeks randomly, so I ignore them). For each week, there is information about two or more featured plants, animals, or events. I have chosen to avoid encyclopedic essays in favor of narrative aspects of lifestyle, behavior, or ecology that are interesting and make for a lively account. Much of this information is taken from the scientific literature, but my own personal observations often play a role. In addition, the text reports locations where you are likely to see the plant or animal described. I confess that, as a resident of central Maryland, I have spent less (but still a considerable amount of) time in western Maryland, the Eastern Shore, and the Washington, D.C., area. Nevertheless, the text should give you a clue regarding where to start on your search.

For each week I suggest a "Trip of the Week," a destination for anyone who wants to experience the best of what the natural world has to offer in the Chesapeake region that week. The choice is obviously subjective, but I have visited each of these destinations (some on dozens of occasions) and have had a wonderfully enjoyable time at each of them. While the focus of this book is Maryland, some of these trips take you a bit beyond the borders of the Old Line State. Each destination, however, is within a four-hour drive of Baltimore and Washington. Contact information is also included, usually as a website address.

Each month includes what I call "Notes from the Field," a chronicle of a memorable experience I've had in unique natural places in and near Maryland. These little essays differ from the weekly units in that they are not constrained by the scientific detachment that normally infuses my writing. The emphasis is on the awe and wonder inspired by nature.

If you have even half as pleasant a time reading this book as I have had researching and writing it, we will both be happy and satisfied. I wish you good journeys, and may your time with nature in Maryland be rewarding, enriching, and enjoyable.

January

Mixed Flocks of Winter Songbirds

It's a cold winter afternoon. Under a bright sun, the forest seems pleasant and inviting. The golden light of late afternoon slants through the trunks of tulip poplars and American beech, casting a filagree of shadows on the forest floor. All is quiet. No call of bird nor trill of insect disturbs the serenity. This quietness is a surprise, for a variety of birds spend their winters in our central Maryland forests: chickadees, titmice, woodpeckers, sparrows, juncos, and even bluebirds. So where are they?

Another ten minutes of hiking reveals a seemingly identical patch of woods, but this one is alive with the chip notes, alarm calls, and drummings of several species of songbird. All of a sudden, the forest seems alive. The birds are moving, always moving, and before each bird can be identified and counted, the flock is gone from sight and out of earshot. Winter birding is like that: most of the forest is bereft of birds, but when one is sighted, it is invariably in the company of a mixed-species flock.

Why might birds of the winter forest form flocks with individuals of other species? After all, during the breeding season most birds are territorial with members of their own species and generally ignore members of other species. The answer likely lies with the unique survival strategies of winter birds.

Golden-crowned kinglets forage in mixed flocks of several bird species in winter.

Winter imposes constraints on birds that spring, summer, and fall do not. Most significantly, food is more difficult to find. Moving across the landscape in the company of a small group means that if one bird discovers a bush full of berries, the rest of the group can take advantage of the bounty, while one bird moving through the forest alone might miss that prime source of winter food.

Another advantage enjoyed by mixed-species flocks is increased vigilance for spotting predators. Cooper's hawks and sharp-shinned hawks—accipiters whose primary food is birds—may find hunting easier in winter, when leaves no longer hide their targets. For songbirds, having more eyes on the skies means that any predator is more likely to be spotted before it can attack.

Finally, some birds, including chickadees and bluebirds, share warmth, roosting together in tree cavities through the long cold night. When it comes time to bed down, birds that travel in a group don't have to search the forest for their bunkmates.

Where to find mixed flocks of winter songbirds this week: Large tracts of mature forest, such as those along the C&O Canal, in Rock Creek Park, and most Maryland state parks often hold mixed flocks of winter birds.

Evergreen Plants of the Winter Forest Floor

Winter can seem a drab season after the bright colors of autumn, but a few herbaceous plants enliven the forest floor with evergreen leaves. These plants tend to be found on dry, sandy soils. Among them are trailing arbutus, partridgeberry, and spotted wintergreen.

Trailing arbutus. This modest plant has thin, leathery leaves, and while many are green, a cluster of arbutus often has some dead, brown leaves as well. Winter is an excellent time to locate trailing arbutus, green against the drab forest floor, so that on a return visit in late March, the small white flowers can be more easily located. Look for trailing arbutus on dry pebbly or eroded slopes. It is often found near mountain laurel.

Partridgeberry. Dark green leaves and bright red fruits make partridgeberry, though small, a notable plant of winter. Each leaf is less than a half-inch across, round, and grows from a long, trailing stem. The scarlet fruits are, as their common name

implies, favored by birds, but a few fruits can often be found persisting as the snow melts away in late winter. Partridge-berry flowers in late May, with paired trumpet-shaped white flowers.

Spotted wintergreen. Another small plant, spotted wintergreen is easily identi-fied by its dark green, leath-ery leaves variegated with white along the veins. While the leaves are slightly aro-matic when crushed, other species of plants given the moniker "wintergreen" are actually the source of the flavoring of the same name. Spotted wintergreen flowers briefly in early June, but its seed capsule, perched a few inches above the rest of the

The cherry-red fruits of partridgeberry brighten the winter forest floor and may persist through the following spring, even while the plant is in flower.

plant on a stalk, soon becomes woody and often persists well into winter. Indeed, the plant's Latin genus, *Chimaphila*, comes from two Greek words meaning "winter" and "loving."

Where to see evergreen plants of the winter forest floor this week: Trailing arbutus favors hilly and mountainous areas and is common along the Appalachian Trail in Maryland, especially near Annapolis Rocks. Partridgeberry and spotted wintergreen may also be found there, but these two plants are also common on the coastal plain, such as at Quiet Waters Park just outside Annapolis. All three plants are often associated with the evergreen shrub mountain laurel.

TRIP OF THE WEEK
First Week of January

Deep Creek Lake area

44 miles west of Cumberland (Allegany County);
just south of McHenry (Garrett County)

What to see and do: It's winter and it's cold no matter where you are in Maryland, so you might as well celebrate the season. Visit Maryland's winter playground, Garrett County and stay in warm pleasant accommodations, but venture out to enjoy nature during the day. Winter sports such as ice fishing and ice boating take place on the frozen surface of Deep Creek Lake, while both downhill and cross-country skiing are available nearby. There are plenty of vacation homes for rent near Deep Creek Lake. For those interested in more rustic accommodations in winter, Herrington Manor State Park, a dozen miles from Deep Creek Lake, has comfortable log cabins that may be reserved. Each cabin comes with a fireplace and all the firewood you can burn during your stay. Blackwater Falls State Park in West Virginia, about an hour's drive to the south, also offers rustic cabins for rent.

Naturalist's tip: Muddy Creek Falls in Swallow Falls State Park, just a few miles from Deep Creek Lake, is particularly dramatic when sheathed in ice, and the surrounding virgin hemlock forest is beautiful on a snowy day.

More information: The website of the Garrett County Chamber of Commerce offers information about accommodations and activities in the Deep Creek Lake area; visit www.visitdeepcreek .com. Information on Maryland state parks in Garrett County may be found at www.dnr.state.md.us/publiclands/western _maryland.asp.

· Week 2 ·

Unusual Birds of Snowy Winters

Folks who feed birds regularly all winter know that bad weather brings in some species not normally seen. Among others, the list might include eastern towhees, hermit thrushes, brown thrashers, and fox sparrows. Most of these species overwinter to our south, but some individuals linger, and some migrate north early. Whether appearances of these birds represent the leading edge of winter territory expansion or are merely anomalies takes years of good data to discern. Also interesting are land birds whose normal winter range is well to our north and who don't normally come to feeders. These birds reveal themselves only to birders who haunt the fields and forests during these short, cold days.

Several species characteristic of open land are found reliably in winter in Maryland, but never in large numbers; shy and well camouflaged, they can be found with diligent searching. These include Lapland longspurs and snow buntings. Although they are normally well dispersed and secretive, a good snowfall brings these handsome birds to plowed road edges, where they are more easily observed. As the snow melts and the first exposed soil is seen along road shoulders, these and locally resident birds are drawn to the only seed sources readily available. When the snow melts sufficiently in fields and forest edges, these birds suddenly become harder to find.

Snow buntings nest in burrows on the Arctic tundra and are a widespread and numerous species there. In winter, they move south and are common in the Midwest, but Maryland's coastal plain is the southernmost extension of their winter range. With white chests and black-and-white wings, snow buntings are both handsome and easily spotted. Hardy birds, snow buntings roost in snow in the lee of a drift and may even become covered during an overnight storm. The snow insulates the birds against

The winter plumage of snow buntings allows them to blend with the snowy winter landscape.

subfreezing temperatures; the next morning, snow buntings shake off their snowy mantle and emerge unharmed.

Lapland longspurs are more discreet in plumage, at least in winter. They resemble sparrows in size, bill shape, and even behavior. Consult a good field guide for identification cues, but any sparrow-like bird associating with horned larks in winter is worth a closer look. Maryland is at the southern edge of the Lapland longspurs' winter range. They move about the land-scape in response to weather conditions and are known to fly, even at night, during a snowstorm. Like snow buntings, Lapland longspurs breed on the Arctic tundra.

Other visitors from the great frozen north are fairly common in some years but completely absent in others. Their episodic appearances to the south of their normal wintering ranges are called irruptions. These southerly movements are largely trig-gered by food shortages. The best-known irruptive species are the seed-eating crossbills, both red- and white-winged, and several raptors, including snowy owls and northern goshawks.

Where to see unusual birds of snowy winters this week: Although the presence of these birds is unpredictable, historically the back roads around Blackwater National Wildlife Refuge, in Dorchester County, and Eastern Neck National Wildlife Refuge and Chester River Field Research Center (Chino Farms), in Kent County, have yielded these bird species. On the western shore of Maryland, small roads in agricultural Frederick County have also been productive.

Reindeer Moss

On a walk across the Maryland landscape, a hiker typically encounters treadways that are hard (rocks), soft (grasses), or squishy (wetlands), but to hear a crunch underfoot is quite unexpected. That crunching sound, as if walking on pretzels, comes when reindeer moss is crushed by a booted foot. Actually a lichen, reindeer moss covers millions of acres of tundra and boreal forest floor in Canada, where it is the principal winter food of caribou. In Maryland, reindeer moss can be found in dry habitats throughout much of the state. In winter, when most vegetation has died back, reindeer moss becomes more conspicuous.

A ground cover, reindeer moss is rarely more than a few inches in height. Its white or gray branches form a dense three-dimensional filagree that is brittle for most of the year. After significant rainfall, the shrubby branches absorb water and become somewhat flexible, subsequently turning a light green as they accumulate chlorophyll.

A lichen is composed of a fungus symbiotically associated with an alga. The fungus provides structure and protection, while the alga contributes photosynthetic sugars that fuel growth of the fungus. Often, both species benefit, a relationship called commensalism. Lichens are more common than most people realize. In addition to growing from soil, as does reindeer moss, lichens decorate tree trunks and rocks, especially at higher altitudes. Lichens secrete acids that actually dissolve rock, the first step in generating soil.

Reindeer moss is rarely used as food by humans. It is starvation fare, used only to "stretch" other foods or as a thickener of soups. It is acidic and may cause stomach distress. However, reindeer moss has traditionally been used as a medicine for diarrhea and is high in vitamins A and B. It also finds use in flower arrangements and as shrubbery in model train gardens.

Reindeer moss is a paradox; it is delicate yet hardy. When crushed underfoot, an area can take decades to recover; and like all lichens, it is sensitive to air pollution. Yet the intact plant can survive and even thrive during the coldest of Arctic winters and through extreme drought. Seeing reindeer moss on a winter walk reminds us that, far to our north, caribou are pawing through snow drifts to find and eat this seemingly delicate little lichen and that it enables them to survive subzero temperatures and icy, howling winds.

Where to see reindeer moss this week: Cranesville Swamp (Maryland–West Virginia border), Soldiers Delight Natural Environmental Area, and Assateague Island.

Gray Squirrels Mating

Round and round the tree they go, first upward, then down, two squirrels chasing a third, the sound of their claws ticking on the tree bark. Gray squirrels are probably the region's most familiar wild mammal, having adapted themselves to life in the suburbs, and even urban parks, wherever large trees abound. This chasing behavior is associated with the two breeding seasons, December through February and May through June. Since a female may mate with multiple males, the mating season involves lots of activity.

Gestation in gray squirrels is forty-four days. Typically, two to four young are born naked and helpless but grow quickly and soon acquire fur. Weaning occurs by ten weeks, but full growth to adult size takes nine months. Squirrels can live as long as twelve years, although mortality rates are high, especially in the suburbs, where death by motor vehicle and electrocution are frequent. Nevertheless, a high rate of reproduction keeps gray squirrels a conspicuous and common resident of many communities.

Gray squirrels shelter in clumps of dead leaves and twigs that they line with dry grasses to provide warmth and comfort. Although they are less active in the winter, gray squirrels do not hibernate; they emerge on warmer days to search for food cached the previous autumn. While winter food is mostly nuts, gray squirrels will enjoy flowers and tender young buds in spring and summer.

Active, abundant, and adaptable, gray squirrels are an endless source of enjoyment for humans. If you doubt their intelligence, just try to keep a squirrel out of your bird feeder!

Where to see gray squirrels this week: Any park or neighborhood with large mature oak trees will likely host gray squirrels. In winter, these mammals are most active on sunny days.

The National Aquarium

Downtown Baltimore

What to see and do: You don't always have to be outdoors to experience nature. January is the perfect time of the year to visit an indoor venue like the National Aquarium. This popular attraction on the water of Baltimore's Inner Harbor features numerous kinds of exhibits, tanks of sea creatures, live animal shows, and a movie theater. Almost 17,000 specimens of more than 660 species are displayed. There are formal education programs for schoolchildren, and for all visitors, docents roaming the exhibit areas are especially knowledgeable and eager to share what they know.

Naturalist's tip: Fish are fed twice a day; try to be present at one of these times to enjoy the excitement and increased animal activity. The rainforest, which is warm and humid, can be particularly pleasant and welcoming in January.

More information: Visit www.aqua.org.

Cranefly Orchids and Anthocyanin Pigments

A walk in the forest at wintertime can be a monochromatic affair; finding a green-and-purple cranefly orchid leaf is a wonderful surprise. This modest member of the orchid family puts out one or a few leaves in autumn and drops them in spring, performing photosynthesis on bright, sunny days during the coldest months of the year.

The top side of a cranefly orchid leaf is mostly green, but it has raised dimples of brownish-purple tissue. The bottom side is completely purple. Because of this unusual coloration, cranefly orchids are conspicuous against the winter-brown forest floor. Cranefly orchids are found mostly in forests on the coastal plain, but are uncommon.

The purple color is caused by the pigment anthocyanin, the same one found in leaves of the familiar houseplant called "wandering jew." Anthocyanins are just one of the accessory pigments, colored compounds that are usually masked by the large amounts of chlorophyll present in most leaves. Only in autumn, when chlorophyll is resorbed, are these accessory pigments visible, giving leaves their "fall colors" of yellow, orange, and red. Accessory pigments have two known functions. First, they

The purple undersides of cranefly orchid leaves add an unusual color to the palette of the winter forest.

absorb light of wavelengths not absorbed by chlorophyll, thereby capturing more of the available light for photosynthesis. Second, accessory pigments can function as antioxidants, scavenging oxygen radicals that may result from photosynthesis in high intensity light. Most accessory pigments are found in close association with chlorophyll, inside the chloroplasts of plant cells.

Some anthocyanin pigments, like those of cranefly orchids, are different. They are found in the vacuoles of epidermal cells, cells that do not participate in photosynthesis. So what possible role could anthocyanins play in cranefly orchids?

One clue comes in the observation that cranefly orchid leaves can often be found with the purple (bottom) side up. After the anthocyanin pigments absorb light, they re-emit that energy as heat. This allows the actual temperature of the leaf to be warmer than the surrounding winter air, making conditions more conducive for the biochemical reactions of photosynthesis to take place in the green portions of the leaf.

Where to find cranefly orchid leaves this week: Mature forests with sandy soil, like those at Tuckahoe State Park and Pocomoke River State Park host cranefly orchids.

Roadside Hawks

Cold mornings in winter often reveal a sight unnoticed in the more temperate months of the year: hawks perched among the bare branches of trees lining interstate highways. Why would these normally shy birds sit in conspicuous view, subject to high-decibel traffic noise, buffeted by irregular winds, in a man-made and seemingly dangerous habitat?

As unnatural as this roadside habitat seems, it holds several temptations for hawks. Primarily, the closely mowed shoulders of the highway harbor high densities of voles, small rodents that

Red-tailed hawks are common throughout Maryland and in winter may often be seen perched in trees adjacent to highways.

look like chubby mice and are a favorite food of red-tailed hawks. In addition, road shoulders are free of human beings (save the odd stranded motorist). Like many birds of prey, hawks are extraordinarily shy of humans, and with good reason, given our species' long history of murder and harassment of hawks. Finally, in winter, road shoulders are often among the first areas free of snow and ice. Is it any wonder, then, that hawks preside over our interstates as lordly surveyors of our peregrinational commutes?

Where to see roadside hawks this week: Interstate 95 between Baltimore and Washington is a driving route that often yields several sightings of hawks perched in roadside trees or atop light posts. In addition, hawks may be seen along almost any interstate highway in Maryland, even along the two metropolitan beltways.

Coldest Week of the Year

Meteorological records for the official Maryland weather reporting station at Baltimore-Washington Thurgood Marshall International Airport indicate that January 12–26 is the coldest part of our year. The average low is 23°F and the average high is

41°F. A majority of the coldest days on record, those below zero, occur between January 17 and January 22. Even so, cold weather is no reason to avoid getting out into the natural world. Dress in several layers of warm clothing, wear gloves and a hat, and walk at your fastest comfortable pace. You'll soon find yourself pleasantly warm. The peace and solitude of "the quiet season" infuse the spirit with a serenity not often experienced at other, busier, times of the year. And while plants and animals may be less obvious, an observant hiker can still find the natural world in winter an engaging and beautiful place.

TRIP OF THE WEEK
Third Week of January

Smithsonian Natural History Museum
The National Mall, downtown Washington, D.C.

What to see and do: A day at the Smithsonian Natural History Museum never fails to fascinate, even if you've visited it many times. Everyone has a favorite exhibit. The most popular displays certainly include the Hope diamond, the dinosaur exhibits, and crystals and minerals. Children will especially enjoy the hands-on items in the Discovery Center and the Insect Zoo. There's a popular IMAX theater inside the museum building as well.

Naturalist's tip: The Butterfly Pavilion, warm, humid, and filled with colorful live butterflies and the flowers they feed upon, is particularly enjoyable in winter.

More information: Visit www.mnh.si.edu.

· WEEK 4 ·

Bald Eagles Nesting

The very first unambiguous sign of spring typically occurs during the last week in January. Several years ago, staff at Blackwater National Wildlife Refuge installed an all-weather camera that looks down on the nest of a pair of bald eagles high atop a loblolly pine in a remote corner of Dorchester County. The female eagle at this nest usually lays the first of two eggs sometime in the last week of January.

Imagine this: spring is six weeks away and reliably pleasant weather even more distant. The parent eagles will have to incubate the eggs without respite for five weeks, from now until hatching, and then keep the chicks warm for a further month or more, well into April. February will be unrelievedly bitter cold, with snow, rain, and wind. Eaglets first fly about eight weeks after hatching; they stay at or near the nest for a further eight weeks or so. This long period of dependency on parental care is the reason eggs are laid so early in the year. The persistence and dedication of these bald eagles make them truly worthy of their role as a national symbol.

Bald eagles are much more common now than just forty years ago and, as the largest local raptor, rule the Maryland sky.

Where to see eagles incubating eggs this week: The Friends of
Blackwater sponsor a website with regularly updated still
pictures of a nest in Dorchester County. Go to www.friends
ofblackwater.org/camhtm2.html. Adult eagles can often be
sighted at Blackwater year-round. See also "Trip of the Week"
for December, Week 2 in this book.

Liverworts

One of the most significant events in the evolution of life on
planet Earth was when plants began to colonize the land. Pre-
viously confined to an aqueous environment, the most primitive land plants evolved a waxy cuticle on the cell surface that
prevented water loss when exposed to the desiccating influence
of air. Later advancements such as specialized gas exchange
cells (stomata) and a vascular system to transport water (xylem)
permitted more extensive expansion onto a greater variety of
terrestrial habitats. One group of plants similar to those earliest
colonizers of land still survives: the liverworts. In Maryland, we
have about seventy species of this little-known group of green
plants. When most other green vegetation has died off for the
winter, liverworts are more conspicuous—if you know where to
look for them.

Since liverworts lack a vascular system to transport water to
all parts of the plant, every cell must be in physical contact with
water to prevent desiccation. Thus, you'll find liverworts in wet
places. Look for them growing on rocks bathed continually in
the spray of waterfalls and just above clear, clean-flowing small
streams. Large streams or creeks that drain developed watersheds rarely host liverworts, because large variations in water
flow leave the plants vulnerable to long periods without a constant shower of water. For this same reason, liverworts are most
often found in shady locations, out of direct sunlight.

Liverworts are primitive land plants found along small streams, where they can be bathed in spray.

In Maryland, the most common species of liverworts appear as green, ribbon-shaped, leaf-like structures (technically called thalli) that are often lobed. The surface may be flat or bumpy. Each plant may have sections of thallus that are black and mushy (due to too much water) and other sections that are withered and brown (due to too little water). Although liverworts may develop specialized structures for sexual reproduction, most dispersal occurs when sections of leaf get torn away and carried downstream, eventually attaching to substrate in suitable uncolonized habitat.

Liverworts are inconspicuous because of where they grow and their stringent habitat requirements, but once you know where to find them they won't seem uncommon. It's always a joy to find these little-known evolutionary revolutionaries that first ventured onto land more than four hundred million years ago.

Where to see liverworts this week: Look for liverworts on shady rocks bathed in the spray from small creeks like those found in Cunningham Falls, Patapsco Valley, and Gunpowder Falls State Parks.

"January Thaw"?

If you've lived in Maryland for a decade or more, you know that every few years we seem to have a "January thaw," a day or two when temperatures rise into the sixties, interrupting that seemingly endless series of frigid days that characterize midwinter. The exact timing of such a thaw varies, but the last week in January is as good a guess as any.

Scientists have actually looked at long-term data sets in search of a statistically significant variation in temperature at the end of January. Their conclusion is that there is no evidence for a "January thaw." There is a great deal of variation in temperature at this and other times during the year; that variation is just not statistically significant. The January thaw is one example of a scientific conclusion most of us prefer to deny. A day in the sixties in late January is merely an anomaly, but that can't stop us from appreciating it. So head outside and enjoy this brief respite from cold weather.

TRIP OF THE WEEK
Fourth Week of January

Polar Bear Plunge, Sandy Point State Park
9 miles east of Annapolis; just north of the western end of the William Preston Lane Memorial Bay Bridge

What to see and do: The fourth weekend in January is the traditional date of the Polar Bear Plunge, when more than 10,000 people brave Arctic air temperatures to fully and willingly immerse themselves in the frigid waters of Chesapeake Bay. It's all to raise money for charity, and the event is well organized and carefully monitored for the safety of plungers and spectators alike. For plungers, it's an interesting first-hand lesson in mammalian physiology. The sudden shock diverts blood away from the skin and extremities. When it returns, there is a well-known tingly feeling on the skin. In some people, the muscles of the chest and diaphragm are shocked into paralysis, resulting in breathing difficulties, including a barking sound upon inhalation.

Immersion in cold water inspires a greater appreciation of wild animals that live and even prosper through long cold winters.

Naturalist's tip: On sections of the beach at Sandy Point away from the human chaos of Plunge weekend, look for a variety of gulls and shorebirds loafing on the beach or soaring over the water.

More information: For more details about the Polar Bear Plunge, visit www.plungemd.com. Information on Sandy Point State Park is available at www.dnr.state.md.us/publiclands/southern /sandypoint.asp.

English Ivy and American Robins

Marylanders have a long-standing tradition of awaiting with great excitement and anticipation the arrival of the season's first robin. In the past, citizens competed to see who would be the first to see one of these familiar birds pulling up a fat worm from the lawn shortly after the last snow of March had melted away. The first robin of spring was a neighborhood news item, just as was the season's first lightning bug, the first ripe tomato, and the first snowfall of the year.

American robins have always been year-round residents of the mixed deciduous forests of the lower Eastern Shore, where hollies, wax myrtles, and other fruit-bearing shrubs of forested wetlands supply abundant food for them. But more and more often, robins spend most or all of the winter in their favorite suburban haunts around Baltimore and Washington. Global warming is the glib explanation. Our winters are warmer these days, with less frequent and lighter snowfalls. But while that might be true, what a bird like the robin needs is food and shelter, not just slightly warmer temperatures.

On a gray midwinter's afternoon, the light fading into a dull twilight, I boulder-hop across a small stream in the forest behind my local community college and walk up the farside hill on a trail created a few years ago by mountain bikers. There's a hint of snow in the air, but it may not be quite cold enough. My boots slide in the unfrozen mud. Up ahead, the normally winter-quiet forest is alive with bird-chatter, and there is continual activity in the tree canopy, as robins flit away from me. It's not the first time I've come across flocks of robins in winter, but there has always been the possibility that they are lingering fall migrants or early spring arrivals. Not so now, in the depths of winter. Even though this is a mild winter, the temperature regularly falls below freezing at night. How can these birds, only a few ounces of fluff and feathers and boundless energy, stay sufficiently warm?

The answer is right in front of me. This patch of forest is heavily infested with English ivy. Almost every tree is coated with a luxurious growth of dark mottled evergreen leaves that rise dozens of feet overhead and protrude from the trunk a good foot or more. This thick mat of leaves and vines provides shelter from the wind and rain, and ameliorates freezing temperatures through the long night. The ivy even provides a midnight snack; dark blue clusters of waxy berries hang from the leaf axils. What a perfect place for a flock of robins, dancing at the edge of survival, to spend the night!

English ivy is yet another non-native plant that has escaped cultivation and become invasive in Maryland forests. Originally imported during colonial times as a ground cover and a climbing vine (what is more traditionally British than ivy-covered walls?), English ivy is still sold commercially, despite the well-known detrimental effects it causes when it escapes its intended bounds.

Where there is sufficient light, English ivy can grow as a carpet on the forest floor, out-competing native herbaceous plants. More frequently, it grows as a muscular, hairy climbing vine, twisting snake-like up the trunk of forest trees. Leaves first appear about five feet off the ground, and grow more densely, extending further outward, with height. A mature forest tree may host English ivy to a height of sixty or seventy feet; only the thinner, more fragile branches near the canopy are spared colonization. The substantial weight of ivy can cause upper branches of the tree to be more susceptible to wind damage. The roots of ivy compete with those of the tree for water in the soil. The many thread-like structures that hold ivy to the tree trunk are adventitious roots that do not conduct water or penetrate the bark but serve merely for attachment. Flowers appear in autumn as globe-like umbels extending outward from the leaves; fruits mature over the winter as waxy, blue-black berries that hang in drooping clusters. The berries are thus present at a time of year when food sources for birds are scarce, and, even though they contain the mildly poisonous glycoside hederin, they are frequently eaten by robins and other birds.

The sun is down now, and in the dim twilight of evening the robins settle into their ivy-covered roosts for the night. For them, English ivy is not the curse it is for trees and woodland wildflowers—and for forest managers and gardeners who strive to grow only native plants. Like predation, competition, and other processes in the natural world, it's all a matter of perspective, of whether you are the one who benefits or the one who loses out. And so the world turns, in this case one more winter's night closer to the more temperate vernal season.

I pick up my hiking pole and head for home, blessed, unlike these robins, with the prospect of a warm fire and a good meal.

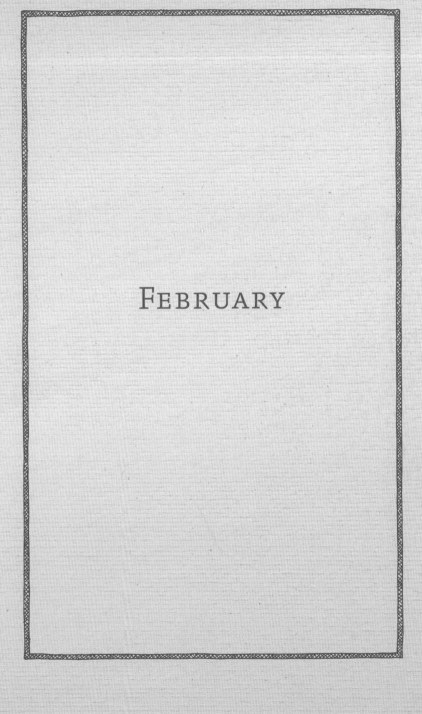

FEBRUARY

Prickly Pear Cactus Fruits

Cacti are commonly associated with the desert, but in Maryland we do have one species: the prickly pear cactus. Prickly pear cacti are more numerous than is generally appreciated, and the species can be found in dry habitats in many parts of the state. Although this plant flowers in late May, its maroon fruits (the "pears") are conspicuously present in winter.

Prickly pear has a recumbent growth form. It is rarely more than a foot tall, but the plants may sprawl over a square yard of sand or stone. The flat, fleshy pads are studded with large spines, but more troublesome to humans handling the pads and fruits are the many short hairlike spines called glochids. Glochids detach easily, can penetrate the skin, and are barbed, so they are difficult to remove. Tongs should be used to handle any part of the plant.

Ripe prickly pear fruits are about an inch in diameter, and a few swollen, maroon fruits typically are found on several of each plant's pads. The fruits are edible if the spines and glochids are removed. The fruit is usually juiced after the skin is peeled away. This juice is often used in candies, jellies, and sweetened drinks. Tender, young prickly pear pads can also be eaten, after all spines and glochids have been carefully removed.

The spring flowers of prickly pear cacti are showy, reaching up to two inches in diameter, and are yellow in color with many yellow stamens. They are attractive to insects, and on a sunny, warm afternoon, each flower will typically be attended by several kinds of bees, beetles, and bugs.

Where to see prickly pear cacti this week: These cacti are often found on sand, as at Assateague Island, Flag Ponds Nature Park, and Terrapin Nature Park. They may also be seen on rocky substrate, such as the shale cliffs lining Sideling Hill Creek and the area near Great Falls of the Potomac River.

Miocene Fossils from Calvert Cliffs

Imagine an ocean populated by great white sharks forty feet long with jaws seven feet wide and four feet tall. It's a scary thought, but about ten million years ago, such sharks lived and died in what is now Chesapeake Bay. We know this because these great whites, and a variety of other sharks, porpoises, and turtles, left their bones to fossilize over the ages in the sediments that are now exposed at Calvert Cliffs. Searching the wave-tossed gravels at the base of the cliffs is a popular pastime with both adults and children. The thrill of finding a big shark tooth or unusual vertebra is considerable; many people enjoy fossil hunting.

In the Miocene Epoch, which spanned the period between about twenty million and six million years ago, a warm shallow ocean covered much of what is now Maryland's coastal plain. The climate was much warmer than now; cypress forests dominated the swampy interface between land and sea, interspersed with sandy dunes backed by pines. Slow-flowing rivers oozed across the landscape before emptying into the ocean. During the Miocene, sea levels rose and fell many times, burying the bones of animals and the shells of invertebrates under successive layers of sand and gravel. Today, this geologic formation is exposed by wave erosion at a number of points around Chesapeake Bay, but nowhere are the cliffs taller and the fossils more diverse than at Calvert Cliffs.

The Calvert Cliffs run along the western shore of Chesapeake Bay from Chesapeake Beach on the north to Drum Point on the south. Winter storms, especially nor'easters, erode the cliffs with wave action. Fossils wash out of the cliffs and ac-

Shark teeth, perhaps the most commonly found Miocene fossil in Maryland, always ignite the imagination of children.

cumulate in intertidal gravels near the foot of the cliffs. The surrounding beaches are the best, and indeed the only, place to look for fossils. Digging in the cliff face is both dangerous and unethical, and it is not allowed. Several people have died while illegally excavating these cliffs. Searching for fossils is especially productive in winter and right after a storm.

Among the animal fossils you might expect to find, shark teeth are by far the most numerous. They range in size from tiny to more than two inches long; small teeth may be found in almost every handful of gravel, but teeth larger than two inches are quite rare. Porpoise and whale vertebrae are also fairly common, as are sting ray plates (their grinding teeth). The shells of fossilized clams, scallops, and oysters are abundant along the shores.

Where to look for Miocene fossils this week: There is no public access to beaches at the base of the cliffs themselves, but several beaches adjacent to the cliffs allow fossil hunting. These include Bayfront Park, near the town of Chesapeake Beach, and Flag Ponds Nature Park (www.calvertparks.org/fpp.html). In late fall, winter, and early spring, Flag Ponds is open only on weekends.

TRIP OF THE WEEK
First Week of February

Flag Ponds Nature Park

11 miles south of Prince Frederick (Calvert County)

What to see and do: The longest and best public beach along the Calvert Cliffs is found at Flag Ponds Nature Park. Search the littoral gravels, along the shore, for fossils like shark teeth, ray plates, and marine mammal vertebrae. Never dig in the cliffs themselves, and use caution when walking below them, as the cliffs shift and portions collapse without warning. You can process more gravel, and thus find more fossils, if you bring along a coarse sieve and a small shovel. You can make your own sieve by weaving wire fencing inside a sturdy wooden frame. Half-inch mesh is good.

Naturalist's tip: The beach at Flag Ponds is also home to the northeastern beach tiger beetle, an endangered species found at only a few sites along the coast between Virginia and Massachusetts. The larval stage lives in burrows on the beach, sallying out to capture small prey that might wander by. The adult tiger beetles can be seen at midsummer during their short mating season.

More information: Visit www.calvertparks.org/fpp.html. For information on Miocene fossils in Maryland, visit http://calvert-county.com/fossils.htm.

Red-winged Blackbirds Return

Perhaps the earliest sign of spring commonly noticed by large numbers of Marylanders is the appearance of red-winged blackbirds, singing vigorously over wetlands. Actually, red-wings are with us year-round; they are merely silent and unobtrusive in winter. Red-winged blackbirds overwinter in huge flocks, feeding by day on waste grain in agricultural fields and roosting overnight in dense colonies in sheltered marshes and woods. By early February, male red-wings disperse over the landscape, select prospective nesting habitat in marshes and ponds, and begin staking out territory with song. Early in the season, male red-wings sing over some amazingly tiny wetlands, like storm water management ponds in the suburbs, that cannot possibly be a successful habitat for raising young. Nevertheless, such sites bring humans and birds into unusually close proximity and make this early rite of spring conspicuous.

Male red-wings defend their territory, not only with their familiar "oak-a-lee" song, but visually as well, displaying their eponymous red (and yellow) epaulets to signal other males to stay away. In fact, biologists have identified two kinds

Red-winged blackbirds can be pugnacious, defending their territories even against human intruders.

of flight displays and five kinds of perched displays they use to defend territory. While chases and even fights do occur, singing and displaying are effective behaviors most of the time for keeping the competition away.

Breeding rarely starts until mid-April at the earliest, when marsh vegetation, especially cattails, begins to grow and green up, providing cover and camouflage for nests. Female red-wings seem to select a territory rather than a mate, and multiple females can nest in one male's territory. The quality of the habitat and its ability to support a family are likely the females' criteria. This seems sensible, since only males with superior fitness are able to defend prime territory. Only after a female red-wing has decided on a territory does she sing. The song is answered by the male harem-master for that territory, and only then does a pair bond begin to form, a relationship that will ensure successful reproduction.

In the red-wings' polygynous mating system, one male's territory can hold as many as fifteen females (but three to five is much more typical). Cuckoldry, initiated by the females, is common, however; often a quarter to half of all nestlings are sired by a nonterritorial male. Scientists believe that having multiple male parents confers greater genetic diversity among the offspring, giving the brood a higher overall fitness.

Red-wings are perhaps the best-studied of all wild bird species, in part because their behavior is so easy to observe; you should be able to find a lone male singing his heart out, even on a chilly February morning.

Where to see red-winged blackbirds this week: Any patch of freshwater marsh may harbor red-wings this week, from tiny storm water management ponds to larger patches of marsh habitat like those at Eastern Neck National Wildlife Refuge, Patuxent Wildlife Research Center, and Lilypons Water Gardens.

Long-tailed Salamanders Breeding

The frigid depths of winter might seem to be an unusual time for a cold-blooded animal to breed, but long-tailed salamanders frequent limestone caves and calcareous springs where water temperatures are fairly constant year-round. Their eggs are laid underground in or near water between November and March, hatching out into aquatic larvae with external gills after two months or so. This predatory larval stage transforms into an adult salamander after three to seven months and becomes sexually mature after two years.

As their name implies, these salamanders have distinctively long tails, which makes them easy to identify; they are the only salamander in the mid-Atlantic area whose tail is longer than the rest of the body. These creatures are very slim, about four to six inches in length, and generally yellow-brown in color. Dark flecks decorate the back, coalescing to form a herringbone-like pattern of vertical stripes along the tail. Like many salamanders, long-tails may drop their tail if bitten or grabbed there by a predator, or even if handled for too long. The tail regrows, seemingly without effect on the health of the animal.

Adult long-tailed salamanders are terrestrial, unlike their larvae, and nocturnal, emerging at dusk to forage on the forest floor. They are most often seen by humans, however, in the twilight zone of caves, poking an inquisitive head out of some thin crevice. While such a thin animal may seem delicate, long-tailed salamanders do very well in their home habitat.

Where to see long-tailed salamanders this week: Caves like Dam Number Four Cave along the Potomac River frequently yield sightings of long-tailed salamanders.

Caves of the Shenandoah Valley

*Several commercial caves are near Luray, Virginia (Page County),
93 miles west of Washington, D.C. There is also a smaller, less commercial cave
near Boonsboro, Maryland (Washington County), 17 miles northwest of Frederick.*

What to see and do: Caves have an important feature that makes
them pleasant venues to visit in both winter and summer: their
temperature is invariant, remaining in the mid-50s. The developed caves in the Shenandoah Valley may be a bit commercial,
with some kitschy interpretations of natural features, but at least
you don't have to crawl through wet slimy cold mud in claustro-
phobic passages (conditions that do not deter devoted cavers).
Commercial caves still give the visitor insight into how caves
form and how they change over time. They provide a window
into a geologic world we humans otherwise rarely see. In the
mid-Atlantic region, caves most often form in limestone where
acidic rainwater and groundwater seep downward to dissolve
the calcium carbonate that is the primary mineral in limestone.
In the cave, slow precipitation of calcium carbonate can form
dramatic structures like stalactites, stalagmites, and flowstones.

Naturalist's tip: If you visit a cave, or any exhibit, ask lots of
questions. Guides do the job because they love the cave or other
subject matter, but after the first few hundred group tours, burn-
out can set in. Even the most jaded guide will come alive, though,
when you show genuine interest and curiosity in the topic.

More information: Among the caves near Luray, Virginia, are Luray
Caverns (www.luraycaverns.com), Shenandoah Caverns (www
.shenandoahcaverns.com), and Skyline Caverns (www.skyline
caverns.com). Crystal Grottoes (www.crystalgrottoescaverns.com),
near Boonsboro, Maryland, is neither as large nor as busy as
those near Luray.

Great Blue Herons Return to Rookeries

St. Valentine's Day is the traditional date when great blue herons return to their nesting sites, known as rookeries (or more specifically, heronries), to begin the breeding and nesting season. While many great blue herons remain throughout the Chesapeake and its tributaries during a typical winter, mid-February signals a change in their behavior. Males gather at traditional rookery sites and begin to refurbish old nests high in trees growing in wetlands. Once the females arrive, several days later, courtship begins. While great blue herons are monogamous for the breeding season, a pair-bond with a different partner forms each year. Eggs are laid in mid-March and incubated for about thirty days. After hatching, the nestlings grow rapidly and fledge after sixty days. Heronries are busy places when nestlings

A graceful flier, great blue herons are perhaps the Chesapeake Bay's most familiar and best-loved waterbird.

are present, providing good viewing opportunities. However, any disturbance by humans or by animal predators, even in the forest around the base of the heronry trees, may lead to abandonment of the nest or cause nestlings to fall to their death. Bring your binoculars so you can observe the herons without disturbing them.

Where to see great blue herons this week: Most herons nest on Chesapeake Bay islands where there are fewer predators and less disturbance by humans, but a few inland sites are well known. Hughes Hollow in the McKee-Beshers Wildlife Management Area along the Potomac River, Piney Orchard Nature Preserve near the Patuxent River, and Mason Neck State Park in Virginia all harbor small nesting colonies of great blue herons.

Yellow Perch Spawning

Spring marks the return of several kinds of fish to freshwater Bay tributary rivers for spawning. The first species to return appears in late February, when winter still holds a lock on the land. Yellow perch have spent the previous summer, fall, and early winter in the brackish portion of the Bay south of the Bay Bridge. They now migrate just a short distance upstream to where rivers are without the taint of salt, to obey the primordial urge to procreate and ensure the future of the species.

Yellow perch have an overall yellowish body and prominent fins that in males are tinged with bright red and orange during the breeding season. Wide dark bands are arrayed vertically over the body, and the two-part dorsal fin has both spiny and soft-rayed sections. Males arrive first, favoring sections of the river that have lots of three-dimensional structure, like submerged branches and streamside vegetation. When the females arrive, they lay their eggs in a distinctive gelatinous strand attached to debris in the river. Males fertilize the eggs in a random fashion, and both sexes of adults are soon on their way back to the Bay. The developing eggs are at the mercy of spring floods, acidic runoff, and sedimentation, but they avoid most predators this early in the season. Larvae hatch from the eggs two to four weeks after fertilization and join the vast throngs of tiny animals that form the zooplanktonic fauna whose numbers expand exponentially as the water warms in spring.

Where to go to see yellow perch this week: Yellow perch are found in most ponds and impoundments around the state, as well as most freshwater tributaries of Chesapeake Bay. Late winter spawning hotspots include Tuckahoe Creek below the dam in Tuckahoe State Park and the nontidal headwaters of Mattawoman Creek, in Charles County.

TRIP OF THE WEEK
Third Week of February

Cross-country skiing, New Germany State Park
27 miles west of Cumberland

What to see and do: Sometimes it's best to embrace winter rather than curse it. A day spent cross-country skiing in often-snowy western Maryland will get the blood pumping and the sweat flowing. A popular destination is New Germany State Park in eastern Garrett County, which has ten miles of trails, some of which are groomed and tracked. Beginners will appreciate the flat, wide trail that runs adjacent to Poplar Lick Run, while more advanced skiers can take on the challenge of several hilly trails on the lower slopes of Big Savage Mountain. There's a warming hut heated by a large fireplace, and equipment rentals are usually available.

Naturalist's tip: Rent one of the cabins at New Germany State Park so you can ski the easy trail along Poplar Lick Run at midnight. Colder temperatures at night often make for better skiing, the winter silence is overwhelmingly peaceful, and the landscape lit by moonlight is surprisingly bright (depending on the moon phase and weather, of course).

More information: Visit www.dnr.state.md.us/publiclands /western/newgermany.asp.

Skunk Cabbages Flowering

It's still winter, but among the ice and snow of forested wetlands, one plant is already flowering. Skunk cabbage flowers are capable of generating their own heat, and that allows them not only to survive cold and ice but also to attract any pollinator insects that might be out and about.

The flowers of skunk cabbage plants look like no other. They are sheltered within a fleshy teardrop-shaped hood called the spathe; the spathe is variegated in color, but dark red dominates, making its appearance reminiscent of raw meat. One side of the spathe has an opening so insects can access the interior, where tiny yellow flowers are borne atop a tee-and-golfball shaped structure called the spadix. This interior space is heated by metabolic reactions of the plant. Temperatures within the plant average an amazing 35 degrees warmer than the outside air. In addition to providing insects with a warm haven, the heat also volatilizes the skunk-like scent of the plant, broadcasting the unique odor through the winter forest. Beetles, spiders, and wasps can be found in the spathe, but early-emerging flies seem to be the dominant pollinator.

Skunk cabbage leaves emerge from the ground later than the flower but are still among the earliest to enliven the forest floor with green.

The spathe of a skunk cabbage appears before the leaves, sometimes poking through snow and ice.

Each leaf looks like an elephant's ear, and by May can be more than a foot in diameter, the better to gather light once the tree canopy is closed. Skunk cabbage is a perennial, with a thick mass of roots anchoring the plant in the muddy soil. By late summer, the leaves yellow and eventually rot away, leaving only a tiny nub of tissue marking where the plant will begin growing the next winter.

Where to see skunk cabbage this week: Skunk cabbage is common in most forests statewide where the soil is wet, particularly along streams and on alluvial floodplains. Calvert Cliffs, Tuckahoe, Seneca Creek, Susquehanna, Gunpowder Falls, and Fort Frederick State Parks are all good choices.

Maple Sap Rising

Is there a purer and more delicious natural product than maple syrup, distilled from the sap of maple trees (primarily sugar maples)? Late February marks the beginning of a very short season when this golden elixir can be harvested. In winter, maple trees store food reserves in stems and roots as starch. Warming temperatures and lengthening days lead to conversion of the starch to the simple sugar sucrose, which rises upward to supply energy to soon-to-be bursting buds. The sap rises over a period of anywhere from a few days to six weeks, depending upon the weather. A typical sugar maple, if tapped, will yield nine to thirteen gallons of sap in a season, and up to three gallons on a good day. This sap is only about three percent sugar, however, and it takes about thirty-four gallons of maple sap to yield a gallon of syrup. In Canada, regulations require that the final product be at least sixty-six percent sugar to earn the name "maple syrup."

Over the last four centuries, the technology for collecting maple sap and converting it to syrup has been improved upon and modernized, but only slightly. In 2009, for example, researchers invented a new kind of tap that prevents backflow and reduces bacterial contamination. The procedure is still very simple: collect the sap and boil away the water to concentrate the sugar. Volatile organic compounds are responsible for subtle flavoring and color (lighter colors are better for eating directly, while darker colors are better for cooking). Real maple syrup is actually rather thin; commercial "pancake syrup," which is mostly high-fructose corn syrup, tends to be more viscous.

Where to see maple syrup making this week: In addition to Oregon Ridge Park (see "Trip of the Week," below), maple syrup making demonstrations take place annually at Cunningham Falls, Swallow Falls, and Herrington Manor State Parks.

TRIP OF THE WEEK
Fourth Week of February

Oregon Ridge Nature Center and Park
11 miles north of Towson (Baltimore County)

What to see and do: Several parks and nature centers in Maryland sponsor demonstrations of the process: gathering the sap, boiling it down, and bottling the final product. It's a delicious way to spend a cold winter day. One of the best places to learn about and experience maple syruping is Oregon Ridge Nature Center and Park, located north of Baltimore. There, park naturalists and volunteers will tell you all you need to know to tap into your own sugar bush during their Maple Syrup Weekends. Oregon Ridge Park, as well as other venues involved in harvesting maple syrup, host an annual pancake breakfast, where you can sample this delicious natural product. You can feel good about patronizing such events, because any profits support the education programs of the park.

Naturalist's tip: Oregon Ridge Park has a network of hiking trails crisscrossing its more than 1,000 acres. The trail along Baisman Run is especially pretty and has many mountain laurels, whose dark-green leaves contrast with the brown forest floor. In the spring it will display a fine selection of wildflowers.

More information: Contact Oregon Ridge Park at www.oregon ridge.org/index.php.

A Gathering of Geese

This gray February day at Blackwater National Wildlife Refuge dims even more by late afternoon, as the cloud deck lowers. Far off, a marsh is burning, and the acrid smoke fills the air with an ashen haze. In the conservation fields, mixed flocks of Canada geese and snow geese graze on winter wheat, a surprising emerald green color in midwinter. Out over the marshes, a northern harrier courses in dipping swoops, searching for an evening meal. And in the tall dead loblolly pine a bald eagle keeps a keen-eyed watch over his domain.

It had been a pleasant day of birding at this mid-Shore wildlife refuge. Great blue herons stood stoic and solitary at the marsh edge, waiting patiently for a cold-dulled fish to swim by. An assortment of ducks—mallards and blacks, baldpates and pintails—dabbled in the shallow impoundments, alone or in small groups. The loblolly pine forest, sheltered from the worst winter blasts, held downy woodpeckers and brown-headed nuthatches traversing the barky trunks in search of the occasional still-surviving insect. Patches of wax myrtle and bayberry held yellow-rumped warblers, flitting actively in search of insects and berries during the short hours of daylight.

Before heading home, I decide to do a "dusk watch" from my car on the westernmost levee. Windows down, heat blasting, I listen to the companionable gabbling and occasional squabbling of geese just across the canal. On the westering horizon, the sky begins to clear, and in that narrow window the sun appears, bathing the landscape in a beautiful clear light for just a minute or two before sinking below the horizon. Photographers will tell you that the best light comes after the sun is gone, so I decide to stay, even as the few remaining vehicles on the refuge stream past me to the exit. The sky, that leaden sky, now begins to blush rose, as the sun, below the horizon, illuminates the undersides of the clouds hanging like wet cotton. Within minutes, the sky is aflame.

From out of the south, a skein of geese approaches, their shouting getting louder as they come closer. The birds behind me in the open fields raise a greeting to the newcomers, who settle gently like drifting leaves among their brethren. The sounds of the geese do not abate; more lines of birds now appear, returning to the safety of the refuge after a day of feeding in the agricultural fields of Dorchester County. Within minutes, the sky is full of geese, arriving from all directions, thousands of them, snows and Canadas both, sweeping low where I can hear the thrum of their powerful wings beating the air, the wind whistling shrill in their primary feathers. The cacophany of yelping, yawping geese increases by the minute, tens of thousands of birds giving voice, drowning all other sound, the incredible noise of life, full of vitality and strength and the promise of the imminent spring migration. I am caught in a whirlwind of geese.

Within minutes it is fully dark, the color of the sky now faded to a dull red ember, and still they come. Tens of thousands of geese overwinter at Blackwater, but only at dawn and dusk can that number be witnessed and appreciated. To stand on a levee with waves of goose music obscuring speech is to experience the natural world as primitive humans must have, with awe and wonder for a planet so rich with life in all its abundance and diversity.

MARCH

Bluebirds Nesting

Few birds cheer the heart like the Eastern bluebird. Is it their lovely song, sounding over attractive habitats like grasslands and forest borders? Or their willingness to partner with humans, who supply the nest boxes this species uses almost exclusively now that most of the natural cavities have been taken over by starlings? Whatever the reason, bluebirds are among the Chesapeake region's most familiar and beloved avifauna.

While some bluebirds overwinter in the warmer parts of Maryland, others are short-distance migrants, spending cold weather in the southeastern states and returning by early March to claim territory and inspect possible nesting sites. By early April, most pairs are sitting on eggs or raising nestlings, the first of usually two broods each year. Bluebirds feed their young beetles, spiders, crickets, and the like, and spend a great amount of time foraging in low grass to keep the hungry nestlings fed. By autumn and into winter, fruits and berries form a larger part of the bluebird diet.

Several kinds of birds compete with bluebirds for nesting cavities, including tree swallows, house wrens, house sparrows, and the aforementioned starlings. While an appropriately sized entrance hole will exclude starlings, house sparrows can be a significant problem for bluebirds, as they are aggressive and will sometimes kill even adult bluebirds. People who monitor bluebird boxes remove nesting

After being crowded out by more assertive birds, bluebirds have repopulated open landscapes throughout Maryland, accepting nesting boxes provided by humans.

material that does not belong to bluebirds to improve the bluebirds' chances. Tree swallows can often be managed by placing a second box nearby, as the two species can coexist happily.

A soft warble of birdsong and a flash of blue through the pale gray branches of the late winter forest are among the most heartening experiences of early spring, and they announce that we can look forward to months of enjoyable observation of this most companionable species.

Where to see bluebirds this week: Many nature centers have bluebird trails, a series of man-made nest boxes placed on poles in suitable habitat near areas of short grass. Several well-monitored trails include those at Pickering Creek Audubon Center near Easton, the Accokeek Foundation at Piscataway Park near Clinton, and Irvine Nature Center near Owings Mills.

Waterfowl Departing

The first week in March is often a time of departures and arrivals for our mid-Atlantic birds, especially waterfowl.

Canada geese are getting restless, moving around more, feeding heavily, and just generally getting ready to go. The "early birds" may depart this week, although skeins of geese heading north will be seen and heard for the next two weeks or so. Here in the mid-Atlantic, consistently warm weather is still a month away, and yet these birds are heading off to the still-frozen tundra of Labrador. Of course, only about half of the Canada geese that overwinter in the Chesapeake region actually migrate; the rest are year-round residents.

Snow geese are leaving now, their long, white, V-shaped skeins a dramatic sight, shining in the sun against a blue sky. Departing from the Eastern Shore, many snows spend a week or two feeding and loafing in the lower Susquehanna River valley

Few sights are more beautiful than a northbound skein of snow geese against a blue March sky, heralding the departure of winter from Maryland.

before heading north to nest in the area around Hudson Bay. Both snow and Canada geese generally move northward at the pace that the snow cover is melting to reveal open ground.

Tundra swans also depart the Chesapeake and stage in the lower Susquehanna River valley around this time. Some have a farther destination than the geese: the northern tundra of Alaska and Northwest Territories, in addition to Hudson Bay. Tundra swans are larger than geese and can also be distinguished from them by their call and their longer necks.

Where to see geese and swans this week: Before they migrate out, large aggregations of Canada geese are best seen at wildlife refuges around the Bay; Blackwater National Wildlife Refuge, near Cambridge, and Merkle Wildlife Management Area in southern Maryland on the western shore are reliably good locations all winter and through early March. Snow geese tend to be more coastal; Bombay Hook National Wildlife Refuge in Delaware is reliable, as is Blackwater. Tundra swans are more dispersed, and large numbers are found only to the south of Maryland. Without a doubt the best place to see snow geese and tundra swans is Middle Creek Wildlife Management Area near Lititz, Pennsylvania, during the first two weeks of March. See this week's "Trip of the Week," below, for details.

Middle Creek Wildlife Management Area

1 mile south of Klinefeltersville, Pennsylvania, and 36 miles east of Harrisburg, Pennsylvania

What to see and do: Days are conspicuously lengthening and cold temperatures are abating by the first week in March. Geese and swans are more attuned to these changes than we are, and they begin their migration northward by congregating at "staging areas" where food and open water are readily available. Such a staging area is Middle Creek Wildlife Management Area east of Harrisburg, Pennsylvania. This small reservoir and surrounding open fields attract tens of thousands of snow geese and several thousand tundra swans for about three weeks each year. As they leave the lake at dawn and return at dusk, the sky is electric with the wild cries of waterfowl. Without experiencing this phenomenon, it's difficult to appreciate how stunning the white blizzard of birds is when they take to wing. When you get chilled in the early March air, warm up by visiting the nature center at Middle Creek, which houses taxidermy mounts of virtually every game bird and mammal found in central Pennsylvania.

Naturalist's tip: The best place by far to view geese and swans is from the Willow Creek Trail, a paved path that leads one-third of a mile to an overlook surrounded on three sides by water. At the terminus of this trail, birds fly low overhead with regularity, and their calls can be almost deafening. Near the trail's end, there are spot-a-pots as well as a shelter in case of bad weather.

More information: Visit www.portal.state.pa.us/portal/server.pt /community/middle_creek/13905.

Wood Frogs Mating

Few signs of spring are more diagnostic, and more ephemeral, than the breeding of wood frogs. On the first several consecutive warm days of March (occasionally even late February), wood frogs move out of the forest and migrate toward vernal ponds, those created by snow melt and early spring rains, where they breed and lay eggs, soon dispersing back into the forest. Their noisy calls alert us humans to the event, but if you miss the right day or two, you'll have to wait until next year. Few animals have such a short and synchronous breeding season.

Wood frogs are most easily found and examined during this brief breeding season, when males announce their arrival at the vernal pond with a distinctive "quack-cluck." The sound is quite loud and can carry for hundreds of yards in calm weather.

The quack-cluck *calls of breeding wood frogs can carry for almost a mile, but the breeding season is short—only a few days long.*

Hearing the cacophony for the first time, some people actually mistake the sound for a flock of passing ducks. In appearance, wood frogs are about two inches long (much larger than the only other amphibian likely to be out and about this early in the year, the spring peeper) and have a distinctive black face mask. It is remarkable that such a small creature can make such a loud sound.

Wood frogs overwinter in the leaf litter of the forest floor. They accumulate glucose and urea in their cells, which provides cryoprotection, keeping their internal water from freezing. Once the soil temperature rises to about 50 degrees Fahrenheit, both sexes move downhill toward vernal ponds. Males usually arrive first and stake out territories by calling and physically driving off other males, but as the breeding frenzy gets under way, territoriality is difficult to maintain. Males climb atop females, remaining in position for as long as twenty-four hours, but other males actively try to displace them. Fertilization is external, and the fertilized eggs are deposited in a mass with the eggs of other wood frogs. Eggs in the center of the mass stay warmer and develop faster.

The developing embryos are clearly visible through a gelatinous coat that slows desiccation. The jelly coat also prevents predation. If you try to pick up a handful of the eggs, they flow through your fingers like quicksilver. Algae sometimes colonize the jelly, giving the mass a green speckled appearance. Hatching occurs in early to mid-April, depending on temperature; while warm weather speeds development, it also may dry up vernal pools, creating an inhospitable environment.

The larvae hatch into tadpoles, which take about two months to develop into frogs capable of living out of water. The new frogs then disperse into the nearby forest, staying in areas with wet or moist soils during summer and fall.

Where to see wood frogs this week: Wood frogs congregate for their brief breeding season in seasonal ponds on alluvial flood plains. Bear Island adjacent to the C&O Canal towpath just downstream of Great Falls and along the Big Gunpowder River near Phoenix Pond are just two of many reliable locations.

Mourning Cloak Butterflies Brighten the Forest

Sunny, warm March days in the quiet of mid-Atlantic forests often yield a seemingly anomalous sight: a conspicuous butterfly fluttering among the gray barren branches and over the brown leaf-strewn forest floor. The mourning cloak is certainly Maryland's earliest large butterfly, and its appearance never fails to delight those looking for an early sign of spring.

Mourning cloaks are generally dark butterflies, with a conspicuous beige border on both sets of wings and on both dorsal and ventral (top and underneath) sides of the wings. A detailed description of its appearance is not necessary, at least not in early spring. It is the only large butterfly around. How can an insect have reached the adult stage so early in the season?

While most butterflies overwinter as eggs or larvae, mourning cloak adults hibernate during the winter months under loose tree bark, emerging on warm March days. During

Mourning cloaks are the only large butterfly to brighten Maryland forests this early in the year.

this time of food scarcity, when there are few nectar-bearing flowers in the forest, mourning cloaks feed on the sugar-rich rising sap, especially that of oaks. At places where the bark is damaged, or where woodpeckers have drilled holes, sap oozes out, providing nourishment. After mating and laying eggs, these aged adults die. Mourning cloaks live for about eleven months, the mid-Atlantic's longest-living butterfly.

Where to see mourning cloaks this week: Any forest of mature trees dominated by oaks may harbor mourning cloaks. Rock Creek Park, C&O Canal National Historical Park, and Patapsco Valley State Park are all good candidate venues.

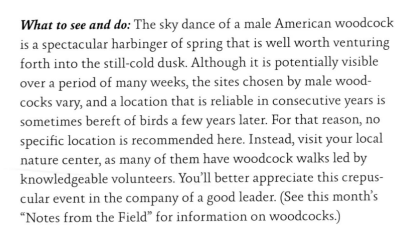

TRIP OF THE WEEK
Second Week of March

Woodcock walks

Woodcocks vary their location from year to year. See further information below for help in locating this year's sites.

What to see and do: The sky dance of a male American woodcock is a spectacular harbinger of spring that is well worth venturing forth into the still-cold dusk. Although it is potentially visible over a period of many weeks, the sites chosen by male woodcocks vary, and a location that is reliable in consecutive years is sometimes bereft of birds a few years later. For that reason, no specific location is recommended here. Instead, visit your local nature center, as many of them have woodcock walks led by knowledgeable volunteers. You'll better appreciate this crepuscular event in the company of a good leader. (See this month's "Notes from the Field" for information on woodcocks.)

Naturalist's tip: Warm, calm evenings are preferred by both displaying woodcocks and the humans who watch them. Auditory cues are important to this mating display, and gusty breezes can make the calls and wing whistles hard to hear. Don't forget to bring a waterproof pad to sit on as you wait patiently and quietly for the display to begin.

More information: Contact one of several nature centers that offer woodcock walks each spring. Check with the Audubon Naturalist Society (www.audubonnaturalist.org) in the Washington metropolitan area, Irvine Nature Center in the Baltimore area (www.explorenature.org), and Pickering Creek Audubon Center on the Eastern Shore (www.pickeringcreek.org). A good source of recent reports of woodcock sightings is https://groups .google.com/forum/#!forum/mdbirding.

Red Maples Flowering

One of Maryland's most common and widespread trees, the red maple, flowers in mid-March (contributing significantly to the first high pollen counts of the year). The red flowers and buds lend color to the still-gray forest landscape. Red maples are found in more types of habitat than any other Maryland tree. From Assateague Island's sandy-soiled shrub zone and the dry ridgetops along the Appalachian Trail, to the fresh tidal swamps of the Eastern Shore and the frost-pocket bogs of Garrett County, red maple has adapted to the full spectrum of soil types. An early colonizer of disturbed landscapes, red maple is now more common than in precolonial times.

Where to see red maples this week: Virtually any wetland, forest edge, or suburban street in Maryland is home to one or more red maples. Patuxent Wildlife Research Center, the C&O Canal towpath, and the Baltimore-Annapolis Rail Trail are just a few of many reliable choices.

Weeds of Early Spring Lawns

Homeowners who treat lawn maintenance as a competitive sport miss out on several colorful plants of turf and waste places that bloom early in the growing season. Perhaps the prettiest is Persian speedwell, whose sky-blue flowers bloom prolifically on sunny days. Color alone identifies this diminutive non-native weed, whose four-petaled flowers grow at the ends of long stalks originating from the leaf axils.

An even earlier bloomer, often flowering as soon as the snow melts in February, is Pennsylvania bittercress, with tiny white

Persian speedwell, the diminutive "weed" of just-greening lawns, is actually a very attractive spring flower.

flowers that require a hand magnifier to see in detail. Look for dark green leaves growing in a basal rosette and an upright flower stem a few inches high. Pennsylvania bittercress prefers areas of bare soil.

Later in spring, a trio of members of the mint family appear: ground ivy, henbit, and purple dead nettle. Ground ivy has blue flowers on a creeping stem and is quite common in lawns. Henbit has reddish flowers and grows in extensive carpets in cultivated early season fields. Purple dead nettle has small purplish flowers and leaves that grow in a conical layered fashion similar to the shape of a pagoda; such a unique arrangement of leaves makes this plant easy to identify. All five of these species bloom early and are gone by late April.

Where to see weeds of early spring lawns this week: Any unmaintained, chemical-free lawn probably has several of these weedy species; check your back yard if you have one and it is herbicide-free. Look for these modest plants in large grassy areas like the campuses of local universities. Fallow agricultural fields like those at the Beltsville Agricultural Research Center also harbor these species.

Osprey Return to Chesapeake Bay

St. Patrick's Day is the traditional date for the return of osprey to Chesapeake Bay, which correlates with the movement of fish into shallow water for breeding. Osprey feed almost exclusively on fish (indeed, they were once commonly known as fish hawks), plunging feet-first for any fish swimming in the top meter or

Fish hawks, or more properly osprey, return to Chesapeake Bay near St. Patrick's Day to reclaim and refurbish huge nests atop channel markers, power poles, and tree snags.

so of water. Upon arrival from South or Central America or the southern United States, osprey quickly pair up and soon occupy old nests or begin building new ones. While newly constructed nests are small, those in use for decades can be truly immense, up to six feet across and ten feet deep. Eggs are incubated for about forty days, and fledging takes place about two months after hatching. Older birds typically arrive a bit earlier, get better territories, use old nests, and have better survivorship of young than do younger adult osprey.

While osprey are exceedingly common around Chesapeake Bay today, the species was endangered within living memory. By the middle of the twentieth century, use of the man-made chemical DDT had become ubiquitous in the Bay area and had caused thinning of the eggshells of many kinds of birds, including osprey. Most eggs were crushed by incubating female osprey, so mortality was high. When the sale of DDT was banned in the 1960s, the osprey population recovered quickly. These birds habituate easily to human activity and accept man-made nesting platforms. Today, a day on the Chesapeake without hearing the chirping of an osprey soaring high above is almost inconceivable.

Where to see osprey this week: Chesapeake Bay and its tidal tributaries host many osprey nests, especially atop channel markers. From the bridge to Assateague Island, pedestrians can look down into a long-established osprey nest atop an adjacent channel marker.

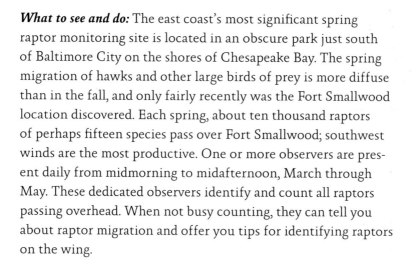

Fort Smallwood hawk watch

12 miles east of Glen Burnie (Anne Arundel County)

What to see and do: The east coast's most significant spring raptor monitoring site is located in an obscure park just south of Baltimore City on the shores of Chesapeake Bay. The spring migration of hawks and other large birds of prey is more diffuse than in the fall, and only fairly recently was the Fort Smallwood location discovered. Each spring, about ten thousand raptors of perhaps fifteen species pass over Fort Smallwood; southwest winds are the most productive. One or more observers are present daily from midmorning to midafternoon, March through May. These dedicated observers identify and count all raptors passing overhead. When not busy counting, they can tell you about raptor migration and offer you tips for identifying raptors on the wing.

Naturalist's tip: Southwest winds are favored by northbound spring migrant birds. Cloudless skies make seeing high-flying birds difficult, while high puffy clouds make better viewing conditions. Bring binoculars and a lawn chair, and dress warmly.

More information: Visit www.mdbirds.org/sites/mdsites/hawks/smallwood.html.

Hepatica Flowering

A modest but very handsome perennial herb of undisturbed mature forests, the round-leafed hepatica is one of our earliest-blooming wildflowers. Despite having a corolla less than an inch across, this diminutive bloom is nevertheless conspicuous, since the forest floor is mostly still a uniform gray color this early in the season. The petals (actually sepals) are bright blue as they unfurl but that color quickly fades to a beautiful pale blue. Within a day or two, the pigments fade entirely, leaving a white-sepaled flower head. The number of sepals is variable but most often six, and the flower has many pale translucent stamens. An individual flower may last only a day, as the sepals are easily dislodged by even a moderate breeze.

The delicate robin's-egg blue of hepatica is a welcome splash of color on the early spring forest floor.

Large tracts of mature forest in central Maryland host a variety of native wildflowers, but the distribution of hepaticas is spotty. Hepatica favors calcareous, basic soils and undisturbed mature woodlands, but neither preference fully explains the unpredictable distribution of this plant. Hepatica does bloom very early in the year, when few pollinators are about, and produces relatively few seeds, which are spread by ants. This low rate of successful reproduction may help explain why hepaticas aren't more frequently encountered. Finally, hepatica leaves were frequently harvested for medical use in the seventeenth and eighteenth centuries (see below), and this may have reduced its prevalence.

Many of our native wildflowers are ephemeral, existing aboveground for only a few months each year. Hepatica is an exception. Its leathery, evergreen leaves persist all winter and may actually photosynthesize on sunny winter days. The three-lobed leaf lasts for one year, while the new green leaf unfurls after seed-set is complete. The leaf soon accumulates anthocyanin pigments, attaining a bruise-purple color for the remainder of the year. Since these leaves are often thin and dry by the time flowering begins, the plant may have scavenged nutrients from the soon-to-be-shed leaves for use in reproduction.

Hepatica got its common name from its resemblance to the human liver: three-lobed and purple. In folk medicine, the leaves were thought to cure liver problems. Herbalists felt that hepatica conformed to the Doctrine of Signatures: God put some plants on earth for humans to use as medicine, and left a clue (a "signature") to its proper use in some aspect of the plant's structure. Modern science, however, has thus far failed to discover any medicinally beneficial compounds in hepatica.

Count yourself lucky when you find a thriving colony of hepaticas. If it isn't spring when you find it, make note of the location, so that you can return on a warm day in late March when these delicate, pale blue flowers nod in the vernal breeze and promise the onset of pleasant weather.

Where to see hepatica this week: Look for hepatica in mature undisturbed forests like those at Gunpowder Falls State Park, Sugarloaf Mountain, and C&O Canal National Historical Park. Locating hepatica in the wild might prove to be a challenge since the species is uncommon. Fern Valley at the National Arboretum has a thriving colony of hepatica, although the plants have been transplanted from the wild. If you visit the arboretum—always a rewarding and enjoyable trip—and see hepatica there, you will find spotting it in the forest easier.

Spring Peepers Singing

In darkness, we scramble and slide down the muddy trail onto the floodplain, where a growing cacophony of sound greets us. The vernal ponds along the Big Gunpowder River teem with activity on this warm late March night, as hundreds of spring peepers call to one another in search of a mate. Up close, the sound is almost deafening. It is a literal orgy of tiny tree frogs swimming, splashing, mating, and fighting, obeying that most basic urge, to reproduce and send your own genes on into the next generation.

Spring peepers are tiny frogs, only about an inch long and weighing less than 0.20 ounce, with a distinctive cross-shaped marking on their back. Emerging from hibernation as the soil warms in March,

Few sounds are more welcome in spring than the loud chorus of these tiny tree frogs in wetlands across Maryland.

peepers make their way to transient ponds, flooded wetlands, and even large puddles and ruts. Males stake out a territory at water's edge and begin to call out a single, high-pitched note repeated up to twenty-five times a minute in order to attract females. A longer trill is a warning to encroaching males to vacate that singer's territory. The "peep" is generated by squeezing air over the frog's vocal chords, which is amplified in the echo chamber of its balloon-like throat sac. A large chorus of singing peepers can reach 120 decibels and carry for more than a mile.

When a gravid female enters a male's territory, he grasps her in an embrace called amplexus and hangs on as she drops eggs singly under vegetation at the bottom of the pond. Fertilization is external. The eggs hatch in a week or two, depending on temperature, and the larval stage persists for another three months, assuming the pond does not dry up in that time. Young frogs disperse into the surrounding forests, joining surviving adults, who can live for up to three years. A major threat to spring peepers is that wetland regulations require preservation of a much narrower forest buffer around ponds than peepers need.

Few common animals are as enigmatic as spring peepers. Because of their tiny size and cryptic coloration, peepers, while easy to hear from a distance, are amazingly difficult to locate and observe; doing so requires great patience and stationary watchfulness. These tree frogs become silent when closely approached; despite being common, spring peepers are rarely seen outside of their breeding ponds. These contradictions conspire to produce a fascinating animal. For some of us, there are few better ways to spend a warm March night than wading around a muddy swamp in search of spring peepers.

Where to see spring peepers this week: Spring peepers can be found in most wetlands, ponds, and alluvial floodplains in Maryland. Among the best locations are those along the Potomac and Big Gunpowder Rivers.

National Cherry Blossom Festival

The area surrounding the Tidal Basin,
downtown Washington, D.C.

What to see and do: To the ardent naturalist, late March brings many signs of spring. For people who may be less attuned to the natural world, however, spring begins with the blooming of cherry trees around the Tidal Basin in Washington, D.C. Indeed, the display of white and pink flowers is nothing short of spectacular. The National Cherry Blossom Festival occurs over a two-week span of time and offers a variety of free events near the Tidal Basin that are well worth attending. Don't be put off by the crowds; the cherry blossoms are justifiably world famous and should not be missed.

Naturalist's tip: Go early in the day to avoid crowds, rent a paddleboat for a unique perspective, and don't even think about driving to the location; take public transportation within the city.

More information: Visit www.nationalcherryblossomfestival.org.

Timberdoodles!

Just the name brings a smile to your face. Almost everything about this bird is comical: its folksy name, its call, its display flight, and its strutting mating dance. Even its physical appearance—a chubby butterball with a long beak, no neck, and wide-set eyes—evokes whimsy. It is more often, but less colorfully, known as the American woodcock. A late March evening visit to its lekking grounds is an unforgettable experience.

The sun had already set and was merely a yellow glow on the horizon as I zipped my winter coat tight around my neck, pulled on gloves and a hat, and walked into a light breeze that, with temperatures in the high forties, seemed colder than it ought. In our area, woodcocks display in March and early April, at dawn and dusk, so watching timberdoodles is often a chilly affair. I hiked a short distance to an open field of grasses and herbs bordered by an area of scrubby head-high trees growing in soggy soil, found a mound of dry sand, and settled in. As the light faded to a murky twilight, I began to hear the strange buzzy calls of male woodcocks—"peents."

At almost full dark, the nearest woodcock began its "sky dance." As he ascended in a wide spiral, I heard a twittering sound, made by air passing over his very narrow primary wing feathers. Near the apogee of his climb, at 200 to 300 feet, the bird began to chirp, and then gently descended, like a falling leaf, still chirping. He landed with a plop and soon began the "peent" sound again.

The purpose of this wonderful and entertaining display is to impress a female woodcock sufficiently that she might mate with the performer. Male timberdoodles are an enthusiastic lot; they begin their displays on wintering grounds before the breeding season starts, continue them during migration, and still make displays long after eggs are laid and young hatched. Maryland is on the northern edge of the woodcock's wintering distribution and the southern edge of its breeding ground, so the season when these displays may be experienced is rather long. Despite all the energy male woodcocks put into wooing and winning females, they play no role in incubating the eggs or raising the young. Their only value to a female timberdoodle is as a sperm donor.

Woodcocks eat mostly earthworms and other invertebrates, probing soft soil with their long, sensitive beaks. Feeding can also look comical, at least to us humans. The bird takes a step, then rocks back and forth, takes another step, and so on. The appearance is that of a chubby disco dancer perfecting a new strut. Scientists believe this "foot-stamping" behavior helps locate invertebrates buried in the soil, similar to the way robins listen for earthworms.

Chilled, I return to my car, pleased to have had the privilege of witnessing this unique and intricate behavior. Coming as it does in late winter, the sky dance of the timberdoodle is one of the surest harbingers of the oncoming spring season.

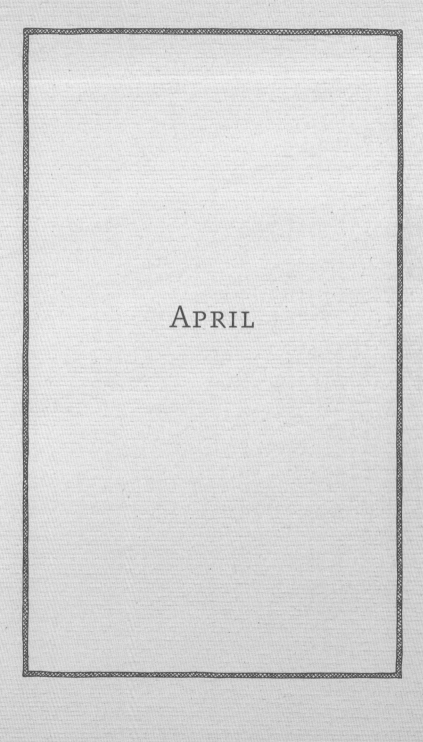

APRIL

· Week 1 ·

Ephemeral Wildflowers
of the Vernal Forest

Two common springtime wildflowers, trout lily and May apple, share a common leaf-production pattern, despite being members of different botanical families. The plants of both species produce just a single leaf in years when they don't flower, and usually only two in the years they do flower. Whether a particular plant flowers or not depends on whether it stores sufficient nutrients in the underground corm (trout lily) or rhizome (May apple). No doubt the second leaf is required to supply the extra photosynthetic energy for fruit and seed development. Both trout lily and May apple are very common plants in forests with rich soils.

Trout lily is most often found on alluvial floodplains, but the species is also present on steep, eroded slopes where competition from other plants is reduced, as well as in pockets of rich soil in the lee of rocks and boulders. May apple is common in upland soils, although it also grows in the same alluvial floodplains as trout lily. The key requirement for both species seems to be rich, well-drained soil in relatively undisturbed forests.

Trout lilies prefer rich, well-drained, organic soils like those found in mature forests. On sunny days, the yellow petals curve reflexively away from the exposed stamens to allow insects better access for pollination.

Trout lilies are small wildflowers with leaves only a few inches long. They often grow in dense colonies and are easy to spot. The leaf is easily recognized—a single fleshy, green leaf speckled with irregular brown spots, like the skin of a trout or a fawn (hence, another common name for this plant, fawn lily). Occasionally the plant will have two or more leaves, and it is these plants that will form a single yellow flower on an upright stem, which originates from the leaf axil at ground level. Plants with only one leaf never flower. The flower lasts for only a day or two, its petals mostly closed on cool, cloudy days but wide open, even reflexed backward, on sunny warm days. It blooms in late March to early April in Maryland; how early depends on how soon a period of warm weather arrives. The flower quickly develops into a bulbous-shaped fruit from which seeds are soon released. The deflated seed pod is gone within a week. The leaves of trout lilies persist only until early summer.

May apples, members of the barberry family, often cover the forest floor like a dense assemblage of green beach umbrellas, connected to each other via shallowly buried rhizomes. The vegetative portion arises from the soil as a single stalk topped by a thick, flat, green leaf with a bit of brown variegation. The only plants that flower, however, are those whose upright stems split into two umbrella leaves. The flower stalk develops from the cleft where one stem branches into two, known as the axil. The showy flower, about an inch across, persists for a few days in late April, and then, if pollinated, spends the next three months developing into a single fleshy fruit. About mid-August, the fruit is ripe, attracting animals and insects alike. By September, the fruit, if not eaten by animals, falls to the forest floor and the plant begins to yellow and die, far in advance of frost.

These two species remind us that many perennial forest wild-flowers spend a majority of their lives underground in a quiescent stage. They emerge to do photosynthesis for only a few months, and flowering and seed set occupy an even shorter period.

Where to see May apples and trout lilies this week: Trout lilies are in flower in early April in metropolitan-area parks such as Seneca Creek, Patapsco Valley, and Gunpowder Falls State Parks, C&O Canal National Historical Park, and Rock Creek Park. May apples are just barely starting to poke through the soil in early April. They will be fully leafed out and in flower by the end of the month in the same parks.

Bloodroot Flowering

Conspicuous on the still gray-brown forest floor are the white flowers of bloodroot. This common and widespread plant of mature forests has an extremely short flowering period, often only a single day. Typically, bloodroot has eight to twelve long, white petals and large, yellow stamens. When the plant is flowering, the single leaf is closed tightly around the stem, expanding only after flowering is complete and persisting through midsummer. Bloodroot gets its name from its orange-red rhizome. The sap

from this rhizome has been used to remove warts, but modern research has shown that the sap's active ingredient, sanguinarine, kills cells indiscriminately and can cause disfigurement of normal skin. In rich soils, bloodroot may occasionally grow in clumps with many flowers, but count yourself lucky if you find more than two or three flowers together.

Where to find bloodroot this week: Bloodroot is usually in flower this week in metropolitan-area parks such as Seneca Creek, Patapsco

Bloodroot flowers last only one day. In keeping with its name, this plant's root is an orange-red color, and a cut stem exudes a sap of that same color.

Valley, and Gunpowder Falls State Parks, C&O Canal National Historical Park, and Rock Creek Park.

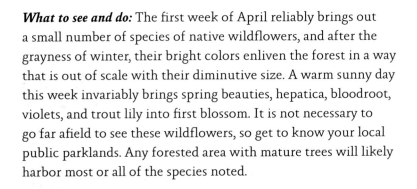

TRIP OF THE WEEK
First Week of April

Wildflowers at your local park

Any park across the region

What to see and do: The first week of April reliably brings out a small number of species of native wildflowers, and after the grayness of winter, their bright colors enliven the forest in a way that is out of scale with their diminutive size. A warm sunny day this week invariably brings spring beauties, hepatica, bloodroot, violets, and trout lily into first blossom. It is not necessary to go far afield to see these wildflowers, so get to know your local public parklands. Any forested area with mature trees will likely harbor most or all of the species noted.

Naturalist's tip: Most of these early spring wildflowers open only on sunny days, and from midmorning or soon thereafter. An early spring wildflower walk is the perfect activity for late sleepers and fair weather hikers. Please do not pick wildflowers; leave them for the next hiker to enjoy as well.

More information: Consult your local nature center. Many of them offer guided wildflower walks in early spring. Another good source of information is the Maryland Native Plant Society (www.mdflora.org/).

· WEEK 2 ·

American Toads Breeding

Joining the chorus of singing amphibians this week is the vibrato trill of American toads. While wood frogs have already finished breeding, and spring peepers have started and will continue for a few more weeks, American toads have now made their way to the same vernal ponds used by these other species. American toad eggs are laid in long strings, making them easy to identify. The eggs hatch in three to twelve days (depending on temperature), and tadpoles metamorphose into adults forty to seventy days later. From that point, toads are terrestrial and do not need to live near water until they are ready to breed. For this reason, toads are found almost everywhere in Maryland: forests, agricultural fields, and even sub-

American toads are our most terrestrial amphibian, living most of their lives away from water.

urban lawns. Only on Assateague Island are American toads missing. There they are replaced by Fowler's toads, which can tolerate the slightly saline waters of the ponds on the island. Surprisingly, American toads do not drink. Rather, they absorb atmospheric water on humid days.

Toads are easy to distinguish from frogs: frogs have smooth skin, while toads have a warty appearance. The largest "warts," found just back of the tympanum and eye, are actually parotid glands, which secrete a toxin meant to discourage predators. Should you pick up a toad, be sure to wash your hands afterward. While the toxin cannot be absorbed through your skin, the sensitive membranes of the eyes and mouth can be affected, resulting in a burning sensation. Yes, toads often urinate when handled. This behavior is another antipredation tactic.

Where to find American toads this week: Almost any temporary or permanent pond surrounded by forest will have American toads from now until the end of April. Listen for their trilling; it is especially pronounced at night but is also audible during the day. Especially good sites include C&O Canal National Historical Park, Rock Creek Park, and Gunpowder Falls and Tuckahoe State Parks.

Early Neotropical Migrant Birds Arriving

Each year, millions of tiny songbirds migrate to and through our area from their winter homes in Central and South America, the Caribbean islands, and the southern United States. Although most of these birds pass through Maryland in late April and early May, a few species get an early start. In particular, pine warblers, palm warblers, and Louisiana waterthrushes are commonly seen and heard here in early

Palm warblers arrive in Maryland earlier than most other migrant songbirds. This early arrival date coupled with their habit of bobbing their tails make these birds readily identifiable.

April. These species have loud and distinctive songs that make them quite noticeable. Since the trees are not yet leafed out, these birds are easier to spot than their later-arriving kindred.

Where to find early neotropical migrant birds this week: While migrant songbirds can be almost anywhere, some sites are more reliable. Look for all three above-mentioned species along the towpath of the C&O Canal National Historical Park, in Rock Creek Park, and along the Patuxent River near the Rocky Gorge and Triadelphia Reservoirs. For up-to-date sightings, check https://groups.google.com/forum/#!forum/mdbirding. For help identifying individual bird songs, visit www.macaulaylibrary.org, which was created by the Cornell Laboratory of Ornithology.

Spring Beauties Flowering

Our most numerous and widespread native spring wildflower, spring beauties dominate the herbaceous layer of many of our forested lands. With flowers less than an inch in diameter, spring beauties make up for their modest size by sheer numbers. A square yard of woodland can have dozens of plants. The combined traits of catholic habitat requirements and the ability to resist light grazing and mowing, mean that spring beauties may be found in forests and even lawns where few other native wildflowers exist. Spring beauties are perennials, sprouting each year from a tuber that is tasty but hard to get at, because it is buried deep underground. The grass-like leaves emerge in late winter, photosynthesizing in cold temperatures when there is abundant light. Individual flowers last only a day or two, but there are several buds on each flower stalk. The petals are pink upon first emergence, but the anthocyanin pigment is quickly bleached to white. Only a pink central line that acts to guide pollinators toward the reproductive structures of the flower remains to give color. While the scent of any single flower is faint, a clump of blooming plants on a warm sunny spring afternoon can be very fragrant. Spring beauties flower throughout the month of April but are uncommon in mid-March and all but gone by early May.

Where to find spring beauties this week: Any undisturbed forest with a mature stand of trees will likely harbor this most common of our native spring wildflowers. Check Patapsco Valley, Gunpowder Falls, Susquehanna, and Seneca Creek State Parks, the C&O Canal towpath, Rock Creek Park, and Sugarloaf Mountain.

TRIP OF THE WEEK
Second Week of April

Great Falls of the Potomac and the adjacent portions of the C&O Canal towpath
6 miles west of exit 39, Interstate 495, Washington, D.C.

What to see and do: Any short list of Maryland venues with dramatic scenery and superb natural values must include Great Falls of the Potomac. Here "the nation's river" crashes over immense rapids, cascades, and waterfalls. Just downriver of Great Falls, the Potomac has carved out a mile-long, vertical-walled gorge for a mile. Far above the river, bedrock terraces have accumulated rich pockets of alluvial soil that create habitat for rare plants, as well as breathtaking displays of native wildflowers. To fully appreciate the area, hike about a mile downstream after visiting the falls overlook. Experienced strong hikers should not miss the Billy Goat Trail, a difficult footpath along the cliff edge that requires rock scrambling and good balance but offers the reward of impressive views of the Mather Gorge. For a more tranquil stroll, use the C&O Canal towpath, where the scenery is more pastoral but historically interesting. Spring flowers are abundant throughout this area. Early-arriving migrant songbirds like blue-gray gnatcatchers, phoebes, Louisiana waterthrush, and pine and palm warblers are attracted to these riverside forests, where abundant water and mature trees generate a diverse set of microhabitats in close proximity to each other. Small vernal ponds next to the canal provide breeding sites for spring peepers and American toads. At mid-April, Great Falls, where nature in early spring is on full display, is an enchanting place to visit.

Naturalist's tip: While spring wildflowers are everywhere in this area, especially rewarding masses of Virginia bluebells are found in the last two hundred yards of the Billy Goat Trail (easier than other parts of the trail), where it links up with the towpath at the downstream end near the Old Anglers Inn parking lot.

More information: Visit www.nps.gov/choh/index.htm.

Rockfish (Striped Bass) Fishing Season Opens

Rockfish, that toothsome and combative gamefish, is now migrating down the Bay along the edges of the shipping channel, after spawning in the upper Bay and tributaries. Striped bass are anadromous fish: mature adults spend most of their time in the ocean but visit freshwater to spawn. About 70 to 90 percent of the entire Atlantic coastal striped bass spawn in Chesapeake Bay, especially in the upper tidal Potomac, the Choptank River, and the Susquehanna flats. The eggs and larvae are susceptible to certain environmental conditions and to pollution. Varying water temperatures cause significant mortality, as does acid rain runoff and trace concentrations of metal ions like aluminum, copper, and cadmium. Young rockfish spend the first three to seven years of their life in the Bay before entering the Atlantic, thereafter returning only to breed. This portion of the fishing season targets spawners returning to the ocean; younger fish must be released when caught. Striped bass can weigh up to 75 pounds; most fish over 30 pounds are female. Larger females are especially important to the survival of the species, as size correlates with egg production.

Where to find rockfish this week: It is possible to catch rockfish from land at Point Lookout State Park and other sites directly on the Bay, but most striped bass are taken from a boat in deep water. For a listing of charter boats, see www.marylandcharter boats.com. For a useful weekly blog about what's being caught where in Chesapeake Bay, see www.dnr.state.md.us/fisheries /fishingreport/log.asp.

Lesser Celandine Flowering

The month of April brings the extensive flowering of this invasive non-native plant in alluvial floodplains and suburban lawns. Indeed, just before trees leaf out, lesser celandine seems to be everywhere, choking out native herbaceous vegetation, including the native wildflowers of April like spring beauty, bluebells, and bloodroot. Lesser celandine has kidney-shaped, thumbnail-sized shiny green leaves and brilliant, shiny, yellow flowers. Emerging from many small bulbs, lesser celandine is almost impossible to eradicate. Only the fact that the leaves are above ground for only about two months, emerging in March and dying back by mid-May, keeps lesser celandine from being considered our most troublesome invasive plant.

The non-native lesser celandine continues to take over both alluvial floodplains and suburban lawns, choking out desirable native plants.

Where to see lesser celandine this week: Unfortunately, lesser celandine is extremely common, even ubiquitous, on the floodplain next to almost every river and stream in central Maryland. It is especially troublesome in Patapsco Valley, Gunpowder Falls, Susquehanna, and Seneca Creek State Parks and in Rock Creek Park and along the C&O Canal towpath.

American Robins Calling at Dusk

Perhaps the ultimate bird of the suburbs, robins have adapted completely to humans and their developed landscapes. Robins will begin constructing nests as soon as the trees leaf out, and by mid-April, male robins are staking out their territories, singing to attract a mate, and chasing each other. Dusk seems to bring the most activity, and their alarm calls and song in the gloaming is a favorite sound of spring.

Where to see American robins this week: Listen for the calls of robins at dusk anywhere and everywhere in Maryland. The only places in Maryland where robins do not nest is on some small islands in Chesapeake Bay and possibly on Assateague Island.

Virginia Bluebells Flowering

Wildflower enthusiasts may argue over what is our loveliest spring bloom, but certainly one finalist is Virginia bluebells. A plant common to alluvial floodplains, bluebells carpet the forest floor as far as the eye can see in some locations. Sky-blue trumpet- or bell-shaped flowers occur in hanging clusters above light green, fleshy leaves. Bluebells are pollinated by bees and butterflies. The flower buds are a gorgeous shade of pink, converting to blue upon full expansion. Albino flowers seem to occur in

most populations. Virginia bluebells have a short season, blooming for only about two weeks in mid-April. Interestingly, while the flower is abundant in the floodplains of some Maryland rivers, such as the Potomac, Susquehanna, and Patuxent, it is missing entirely from others, like the Patapsco.

Virginia bluebells form natural gardens covering many acres of alluvial floodplains at several locations in central Maryland.

Where to find Virginia bluebells this week: Extensive stands of bluebells occur at Susquehanna State Park, along the C&O Canal towpath, at Patuxent Research Refuge (North Tract), and at Bull Run Regional Park (Virginia).

TRIP OF THE WEEK
Third Week of April

Susquehanna State Park
8 miles north of Havre de Grace (Harford County)

What to see and do: The alluvial floodplains of the Susquehanna River are home to an amazing and beautiful display of Virginia bluebells. A natural garden about a mile long and up to one hundred feet wide, almost all of it covered in bluebells, is located on the isthmus just upstream of where Deer Creek dumps into the Susquehanna River. There are other wildflowers in abundance here as well, including trillium, spring cress, wild ginger, spring beauties, wild geranium, and May apples. The forest is alive now with early migrating songbirds, although they are not nearly as plentiful as they will be in a week or two; the nearby picnic area is often very productive for warblers.

Naturalist's tip: Growing abundantly on the hillsides overlooking the floodplain is another beautiful and uncommon wildflower, red trillium. However, here in Susquehanna State Park, the petals of this trillium are white, rather than the usual deep crimson color. This robust plant, about a foot high, is quite beautiful, and it flowers at the same time as the bluebells.

More information: Visit www.dnr.state.md.us/publiclands/central /susquehanna.asp.

· WEEK 4 ·

Canopy Closure

The most significant ecological event of the year is canopy closure, when trees put out their leaves, shading the forest floor and beginning the season of photosynthesis. While a few trees leaf out earlier, canopy closure is a relatively synchronous event that occurs early in the last week of April, year in and year out. With the resulting sharp decline in light on the forest floor comes a decline in the number and variety of vernal ephemeral wildflowers. Shade-tolerant plant species begin to grow. Insect populations increase dramatically to feed on the tender young leaves and buds. Migrating warblers arrive to feed on this insect feast, filling the forest with song. Nesting starts, since the new leaves will hide nests from predators. Ground-level humidity increases, and soil temperatures are buffered against the heating that will accompany increasing seasonal air temperatures. River levels drop rapidly as trees take up the soil water they need for growth. Indeed, the implications of canopy closure for the ecology of forests, woodlots, and shaded residential areas can hardly be overestimated.

Lyre-leaved Rock Cress Flowering

Soldiers Delight Natural Environmental Area is a large and mostly intact serpentine barren, an unusual type of ecosystem where the soil contains a high concentration of serpentine metals, such as chromium. Several dozen rare plants grow in this unique habitat, and late April finds one of the most prolific in flower, the lyre-leaved rock cress. While not the most colorful or rare plant at Soldiers Delight, this diminutive wildflower carpets the rocky barrens in breathtaking abundance.

Lyre-leaved rock cress grows profusely at Soldiers Delight Natural Environmental Area, even on stony substrate where the only soil is what accumulates in cracks in the rocks.

Lyre-leaved rock cress is a member of the mustard family, with four white petals atop a very thin stem. It grows between cracks in the rock, in thin crevices that have accumulated the slightest bit of nutrient-poor soil. Leaves grow in a basal rosette that lies directly on the substrate; in summer, this hardy plant somehow endures temperatures that could fry an egg. Each leaf is deeply lobed and appears like the neck of the stringed instrument from which its name derives. The leaves persist over the winter and likely do most of their photosynthesis on warm winter and early spring days.

Where to see lyre-leaved rock cress this week: Soldiers Delight Natural Environmental Area.

Morel Mushrooms Ready for Harvest

Late April is typically the prime season for collecting one of nature's finest delicacies: morel mushrooms. These tasty wild mushrooms grow in mature forests with a well-developed and

Morels are perhaps the most gastronomically desirable food that can be gathered from the wild in Maryland.

complex leaf litter and top soil. Nevertheless, they blend well with last winter's dead leaves, and are difficult to find except to the experienced eye. Once found and harvested, they can be eaten fresh by sautéeing with butter, or dried for later reconstitution and consumption.

Eating wild mushrooms can be a risky proposition unless you are knowledgeable regarding how to distinguish the edible from the poisonous. Morels, however, are quite singular in appearance and are difficult to mistake. Most are a few inches tall, phallic in shape, and spongy or honeycombed in appearance. They are hollow inside, so it takes a lot of morels to make a pound. The flavor of morels is robust and often described as "meaty" or "earthy."

Every mushroom hunter has his or her own particular theory of where to look for morels. Most seem to agree that the mushrooms are associated with mature forests dominated by tulip poplar, ash, beech, or oaks. Look around the drip line of these large trees (the perimeter of the area sheltered by a tree). Among forest herbs, morels are sometimes found in the same location as May apples. Long cool wet springs often yield a fine harvest.

What we see above ground for short periods of time and call a mushroom is actually the spore-bearing fruiting body of a fungus. Soil fungi consist of long-lived, thread-like mycelia that form a mesh-like network in soil and leaf litter, absorbing nutrients for growth that are released during the decay process. Fungi play an important but often poorly appreciated role in soil ecology and nutrient cycling.

Where to find morels this week: Rock Creek Park, C&O Canal National Historical Park, and Catoctin Mountain Park are acknowledged morel hot spots, but almost any mature forest with a good leaf litter accumulation statewide holds possibilities.

Redbuds and Dogwoods

Among the glories of our wondrous spring season are two small trees that display beautiful, showy flowers just before most trees leaf out. Eastern redbuds and flowering dogwoods are both understory trees that rarely grow to more than 25 feet in height, do well in a mix of sun and shade, and are distributed through much of the eastern half of the United States. Both are native species that are often planted as ornamentals. Redbuds, more tolerant of poor soils and environmental insults than dogwoods, are frequently planted along roadways, where their bright magenta flowers make a spectacular display in mid- to late April.

Dogwoods are especially popular with homeowners, who often plant them singly, as a focal point for their lawn or garden.

Redbuds are legumes; they have the ability to extract nitrogen from the air and, in partnership with soil bacteria, convert that nitrogen into usable forms. So, while most plants must scavenge nitrogen from soil, where it is often rare, redbuds

The striking magenta flowers of redbuds may grow anywhere on the entire length of the woody branches, and even directly from the tree's trunk.

produce their own supply of nitrogen fertilizer. The colorful flowers make identification of this tree easy. The flowers grow in clusters from branches and even the main trunk. The fruit is a long, flat, brown pod that holds the seeds. Few birds are able to open these pods, so redbud seeds are rarely consumed by birds. The leaves are distinctly heart-shaped. Redbuds are hardy trees that are resistant to most diseases.

Dogwoods have sparse branches and twisted limbs. Most trees are too small to produce commercially useful wood, but there is some demand for larger specimens for specialty uses, including loom shuttles, golf club heads, tool handles, and as inlays and veneers. The flowerheads are quite large, several inches across, consisting of four white petal-like bracts, each with a rust-colored stain at the tip. About twenty tiny individual flowers cluster at the center. The fruits turn bright red in September, when they are eaten by many species of birds. Robins in particular decimate the fruits of dogwoods in the suburban habitat they share, and gray squirrels scavenge whatever the robins leave behind. Unlike redbuds, dogwoods are susceptible to a variety of diseases. The most deadly is the anthracnose fungus, which in the last twenty years has killed a high percentage of wild dogwood trees throughout Maryland.

Redbuds and dogwoods both have a place in American Christian folklore. Supposedly, Judas Iscariot, who betrayed Jesus, later hanged himself from a redbud tree; the magenta color of the flowers reminds Christians of this blood crime. American colonists explained several characteristics of dogwoods by proposing that Jesus was crucified on a cross made of dogwood, which, according to the legend, was a straight tree at the time but thereafter grew twisted. The flower reminds Christians of the crucifixion: the petals (bracts) are in the shape of a cross, each with an indentation and the stain of a rusty nail at the edge, while the central flowerhead looks similar to a crown, reminiscent of thorns placed on Jesus's head.

Where to see redbuds and dogwoods this week: The hot pink flowers of redbud stand out in greening forests. In addition, redbuds are frequently planted along roadsides. Dogwoods are still common, especially on suburban lawns, but wild dogwoods are more rare than in the past. They have been virtually eradicated in Catoctin Mountain Park and some other places where they were once a common understory tree. Wild and domestic varieties of dogwood can also be seen at the National Arboretum (see below).

TRIP OF THE WEEK
Fourth Week of April

The National Arboretum

Northeast Washington, D.C.

What to see and do: A visit to the National Arboretum in Washington is wonderful at any time of year, but the end of April is certainly the best. This is azalea season, and more than 50,000 plants in every color of the rainbow dot a partially shaded hillside in the western section of this undeservedly obscure national treasure. The show is nothing short of spectacular. But azaleas are not the whole story. The dogwood collection is in its full-blooming glory this week as well. Fern Valley, a collection of native wildflowers in a natural forest setting, is also near prime now, and the Asian collections are always of interest. No matter what the time of year, the National Arboretum is an enchanting place to visit.

Naturalist's tip: There's more to see than plants in flower at the National Arboretum. Don't miss the National Bonsai Museum, the National Herb Garden, and the very photogenic National Capitol Columns.

More information: Visit www.usna.usda.gov.

The Wildflowers of April

April is the best month for viewing native forest wild-flowers, and I've come to a site on the Appalachian Trail in northern Virginia to see a spectacular display of large-flowered trillium and other short-lived plants of the vernal season. Botanists and wildflower enthusiasts love the flora of April for any number of reasons: they are the first flash of life and color after a long dull winter; many of these flowers are so ephemeral that to catch them at the peak of bloom is a challenge; and many species grow best in an increasingly rare habitat, large tracts of mature forests not yet heavily affected by invasive non-native plants. On this day in late April, the sun is shining, the sky is blue, and the birds are singing—trite, I know, but some days afield really are like this; and mind, body, and soul rejoice with thanksgiving for the gift of life.

I start down a rocky trail in a dense forest not yet fully leafed out. The upper branches of trees bear a lime-green fuzz of tiny leaves that in another week will expand completely and cast a deep shade. Today, however, the low herbs of the forest floor are prospering in full sun, hustling to complete their reproductive cycle of flower and fruit and seed dispersal while photosynthesizing in these few days of optimal light and springtime warmth. I stop to listen. In the quiet between breezes, a low hum fills the air, insects in search of pollen and nectar, unwittingly fulfilling the need of immobile plants to spread their genetic heritage afar.

Large-flowered trillium are everywhere, growing in the rich organic soil in a density of several plants per square foot. Each flower, initially shaped like the bell of a trumpet, emerges from the center of a whorl of three leaves atop a stem a few inches to a foot in height. It's a simple but elegant flower that comes in a graded series of shades of pink, from magenta to pink to pale pink to white. Deep in the center are six pale stamens bearing yellow pollen, and a greenish-yellow, tripartite pistil awaiting fertilization. Each flower is three to four inches across, giving the species both its common and Latin specific names, *large-flowered* and *grandiflorum*, respectively.

Other wildflowers are common here as well. May apples grow in clusters, their deep green umbrella-shaped leaves forming a short canopy only a foot high. Many are flowering, bearing an inch-wide disk of white petals with prominent pistil and stamens located below the leaves. Wild geraniums, too, are widespread, with beautiful five-petaled purple flowers. Taken together, these three species cover the forest floor in a density rarely seen in parks and preserves close to metropolitan areas like Washington and Baltimore.

In fact, this forest appears remarkably different from those we urban dwellers know. In addition to the rich herb layer, there are plenty of shrubs and saplings. In another few weeks, it'll be impossible to see more than a few yards into the forest, as these understory plants leaf out. Remarkably, in a mile of hiking I see only one non-native plant, a scrawny specimen of garlic mustard that I pull up and discard. There's no Japanese stiltgrass, no barberry, no lesser celandine, all invasive alien plants commonly seen in forests near population centers. In some small part, this is due to the isolation of this tract of land, the relatively little human visitation it sees during most of the year. But in large measure, the complex multilayered character of this forest, and the rich understory of spring wildflowers, is due to a low density of whitetail deer.

Seventy years ago, whitetail deer were rare, their numbers having been greatly reduced by subsistence hunting. The establishment of hunting regulations permitted deer populations to increase, and today many central Maryland parks have deer densities up to ten times higher than is desirable. We have become used to forests that have native herb and shrub layers grazed back to stubs, and saplings that have been nibbled out of existence. And it's not just the flora that is affected by over-grazing of whitetail deer. Without a significant herb, shrub, and sapling layer, bird populations have been declining as well. Species like wood thrushes, Kentucky warblers, ovenbirds, and hooded warblers have disappeared from deer-infested wood-lands. Even forest insects have been affected. Deer ticks, which often feed on the blood of deer, are far more common today than they were fifty years ago. There are still large canopy trees in metropolitan-area woodlands, but the forest as a whole is a pale imitation of its former self.

Hiking back to the car, I marvel at the extensive carpet of wildflowers and the abundance of birdsong in this forest where whitetail deer are scarce. Many of us have forgotten what an intact forest looks and sounds and feels like, our expectations having been unconsciously lowered by several decades of slow depletion of vegetation density and diversity. Will future gen-erations remember at all, or will the inertia of lowered expecta-tions become the new normal? The decisions our society makes about whitetail deer will largely determine the answer.

MAY

Azaleas Flowering

Azaleas are the glory of springtime Maryland, and most hybrid varieties are at their peak this week, in the midst of lawns and gardens. Several species of wild azalea are also blooming, but they tend to be more modest, with flowers placed less densely along the stems. Branches of wild azaleas are often "leggy" as they reach for light, unlike the compact bushy plants typical of domestic varieties. In the wild, look for azaleas on dry, well-drained soil. Like other members of the heath family, they prefer the dry side of the soil moisture spectrum (the exception is swamp azalea). In the Piedmont, the most common species is Pinxter-flower azalea. "Pinxter" is a Dutch word referring to Pentecost, fifty days after Easter, not a good way to mark blooming, given the variation in the date of Easter. Azaleas flower far more predictably. This species of azalea has five long, pink stamens that extend beyond the petals, and a single red pistil that protrudes even farther, allowing pollination by large insects such as butterflies. The flowering dates of azaleas from Florida to New England match the northward progression of migrating ruby-throated hummingbirds, implying that these tiny birds depend on the nectar of wild azaleas.

Where to see azaleas this week: Wild azaleas are rarely present in large stands, but they can often be found singly and in association with mountain laurel. Look for them in Gunpowder Falls, Tuckahoe, and Pocomoke River State Parks. For incredible displays of domestic varieties, don't miss the National Arboretum.

Yellow Lady's Slipper
Orchids in Bloom

The first week in May is prime time for the short flowering season of one of Maryland's most beautiful and unusual wildflowers, yellow lady's slipper orchids. Unlike the fairly common pink lady's slipper, yellow lady's slipper orchids require undisturbed mature forest with rich, well-drained soils and a thick layer of leaf mold and other organic materials. The long, shallow roots need the high oxygen levels of this humus-rich soil, but shallow roots are also susceptible to damage. While it was once thought that these roots required a symbiotic relationship with fungi of the genus *Rhizoctonia*, recent research indicates that the fungus is probably necessary only at the seedling stage. Lady's slipper plants can live for a century, but they may flower in only ten to twenty of those years and set seed in only two or three. These orchids are clearly adapted to an undisturbed habitat and are in it for the long haul!

Yellow lady's slipper orchids have uniquely shaped flowers. The species is rare in Maryland.

Where to see lady's slipper this week: Yellow lady's slippers are very rare in central Maryland, and their locations are usually a secret well kept by the naturalists who try to protect them. At Thompson Wildlife Management Area, near Front Royal, Virginia, there is a larger and easier-to-find population. Pink lady's slipper orchids are often found in dry soil under an oak-pine canopy. Tuckahoe and Pocomoke River State Parks and the Appalachian Trail harbor healthy populations that bloom in late April.

Prothonotary Warblers Return

Of all the species of warblers nesting in Maryland, probably none is easier to see and enjoy than the prothonotary warbler. Of course, you have to go to the right habitat: wooded swamps on the Coastal Plain. To see them, you'll need to access these swamps by canoe, but once there, prothonotaries are conspicuous—they stay low to the water, avoiding the treetops; they are brightly colored; they sing persistently and loudly; they are very active; and they seem unafraid of humans.

When these golden birds arrive from the tropics, usually in the last few days of April or the first few days of May, the males immediately begin staking out territories along the river, singing conspicuously, and aggressively chasing rival males. Those first few days are chaotic until territories are well established. In Maryland, prothonotaries are most common along bald cypress–lined rivers like the Pocomoke, where territories seem as regularly spaced as houses in the suburbs. The density of territories is greatest where the tree canopy closes over the river.

Once the females arrive and choose a mate, nest building gets quickly under way. Prothonotaries are unusual among birds in that they nest in tree cavities, although they will accept man-made nest boxes similar in size to bluebird boxes. Each territory usually contains one or more possible nest sites that the male shows to the female. Once she

Active and brilliantly plumaged, prothonotary warblers enliven wooded swamps on Maryland's coastal plain.

selects one, they line it with moss, and egg laying begins within a few days. On average, the clutch size is five eggs. Hatching occurs after about two weeks of incubation, and the young fledge in about eleven days. A second brood is sometimes raised in the same breeding season. Unlike many species of warblers, prothonotaries are doing well in Maryland and are not declining in numbers.

Where to see prothonotary warblers this week: The Pocomoke River watershed is the best place to see prothonotaries. A canoe trip on the Pocomoke or its tributaries, Nassawango Creek, Corkers Creek, and Dividing Creek, will yield dozens of sightings. Closer to central Maryland, the wooded swamps of Tuckahoe Creek and the Patuxent River are usually productive. Also look along the tidal Potomac River and upstream as far as Harpers Ferry in the big, riverside silver maples.

Large-flowered Trillium in Bloom

Few of our native forest wildflowers are as striking as large-flowered trillium. Found primarily in mountainous areas such as the Blue Ridge and Appalachian plateau, these robust plants often grow in colonies that dominate the forest floor. Trilliums are easily recognized; they have three large leaves, three white petals, and three pale green sepals on a large white funnel-shaped flower.

Large-flowered trilliums are long-lived perennials. In fact, a plant is seven to ten years old before a flower appears, and germination of the seed requires two winters. This slow-growing plant must reach a critical size before it has the resources to flower and set seed; there must be at least 5.6 square inches of leaf and at least 0.15 cubic inches of rhizome to permit flowering. Mature fruits contain on average just sixteen seeds. These

Large-flowered trilliums are beautiful and common wildflowers in mountainous terrain. The petals are often entirely white in color, although some populations display varying amounts of pink in their petals.

seeds are spread by both ants and whitetail deer. Each seed has an elaiosome, an oil-rich appendage that attracts insects. Ants carry the seed back to their burrow, where the seed eventually germinates and grows in its own bed of rich, well-aerated soil.

Whitetail deer compete with ants for trillium seeds. Large-flowered trillium is a favorite food of deer, who will eat this plant in preference to all others. In moderation, the herbivory of deer is useful, as it spreads the seeds over larger distances than ants can. Since many forested areas now have excessively high numbers of whitetail deer, large-flowered trilliums have become less numerous and are even rare in some locations. Even where trilliums are not killed by overgrazing, they will grow shorter each year, since they have fewer resources to put into growth, and they might never flower. The height of trillium plants correlates inversely with the size of the local deer population.

Humans have had an impact on large-flowered trilliums as well. *Trillium grandiflorum* is one of the most common native forest wildflowers sold by garden centers, often as a naked rhizome. Yet most of these plants never grow, or they die after only a year. Transplantation of the adult plant is equally fraught with difficulty. So enjoy large-flowered trillium in its native habitat rather than trying to plant it in your garden.

Where to see large-flowered trillium this week: Thompson Wildlife Management Area (see "Trip of the Week" below).

Thompson Wildlife Management Area

15 miles east of Front Royal, Virginia (Fauquier County)

What to see and do: Spring comes later to the mountains, so when the leaf canopy has closed in forests near Washington and Baltimore, trees in the Blue Ridge are just starting to green up. Consequently, in the mountains the spring ephemeral wild-flower season is still in full swing in early May. Perhaps the most amazing display of these beautiful wildflowers is at Thompson Wildlife Management Area near Front Royal, Virginia. Large-flowered trillium in particular is present in abundance, covering the forest floor in an astonishing profusion. Other common species in full flower this week include May apple, wild geranium, and several kinds of violets.

Naturalist's tip: Many species of neotropical migrant songbirds are passing through the mid-Atlantic this week. While trees in central Maryland have fully leafed out, in the mountains the trees are still mostly bare, circumstances that make locating and viewing these small, active birds easier. So, take along your binoculars.

More information: Visit www.dgif.virginia.gov/wmas/detail.asp?pid=31.

Black Locusts in Flower

The flowers of black locust trees are remarkably fragrant, but not many people take the opportunity to appreciate the delicate scent of *Robinia pseudoacacia*. Bees, however, know the value of black locust flowers and collect nectar during its brief blooming season in early May. That sparsely leafed, somewhat twisted tree with clouds of creamy white blossoms found lining most highways in central Maryland is black locust.

Black locust flowers have a lovely scent that attracts many honeybees during the tree's short blooming season.

One of two common trees found in Maryland bearing the epithet "locust," black locusts lack the thorns found on the trunk and branches of honey locusts. Black locust is a member of the pea family, and its roots have the ability to obtain nitrogen from the air through a symbiotic relationship with certain bacteria. For this reason, black locust grows well in poor or disturbed soils and has colonized the far edge of highway shoulders that are often bulldozed free of topsoil during road construction.

The wood of black locust is very hard and burns without smoke, making it popular for use in woodstoves. It is also rot-resistant and will last more than a century in the ground when used as a fencepost. Abraham Lincoln, the railsplitter of lore, likely did much ax-work on black locust.

Where to see black locust this week: Black locust is quite distinctive when flowering. Look for its pendulous clusters of white flowers on trees lining Interstates 70 and 95, as well as many other highways and smaller roads in central Maryland. It is also a popular street tree in cities and towns.

Fantail Darters Breeding

Among the animals with which we share Maryland, few are more common than a little-known fish called the fantail darter. A resident of small, riffle-strewn streams, this two-inch long member of the perch family is atypical in that it tolerates somewhat degraded water quality, including low oxygen levels, warm temperatures, and siltation. An unusual reproductive strategy has elevated the fantail darter's once-humble status to a higher level and has brought it to the attention of evolutionary biologists.

Fantail darters are common but often overlooked residents of small, clean streams in central Maryland. They have the ability to change color when interacting with other darters.

There are about 150 species of darters in the United States, eleven of which are found in Maryland. Some members of this diverse clan are exceedingly rare, like the possibly extinct Maryland darter, while others are quite common. All are less than six inches long, and many darters occupy the streambed rather than the water column. They move rapidly (darting) over the gravelly substrate of riffles, eating primarily aquatic insects and other small benthic (bottom-dwelling) animals.

While some darters are brightly colored, fantails are a dull yellowish brown with dark tiger-like stripes. The dorsal fin is in two parts: the anterior portion is short and spiny while the posterior portion is a more typical fin. During the breeding season, the head of the male gets darker, but fantails do not exhibit the dramatic breeding season changes in coloration that many other darter species exhibit.

Fantail darters begin breeding once water temperatures have warmed sufficiently. A male clears out silt from an area under a flat rock, leaving just enough space to get his body into the cavity. The female lays her eggs singly on the roof of this nest, ovipositing from an inverted position. The male fertilizes the eggs in place. More than one female may deposit eggs in one male's nest. The male attracts females by placing his anterior dorsal fin against the nest roof. Each spine of the fin is tipped with a round structure that mimics a fantail egg; a female is attracted by this (false) advertisement that the male has already bred successfully.

Where to find fantail darters this week: Fantails, like all darters, are inconspicuous, but you will see them once you know where and how to look. Headwater streams of the Monocacy and Patapsco Rivers contain fantail darters. For information on distribution of darters and other stream fauna, see the Maryland Biological Stream Survey (www.dnr.state.md.us/streams/MBSS.asp).

May Worm Jubilee

Few creatures in Chesapeake Bay are more obscure than the small worms that live in muddy bottom sediments, yet these polychaete worms are an important part of the food chain and play a significant role in the ecology of the Bay. One species, the common clamworm (*Nereis succinea*), becomes conspicuous for a few days each May when huge numbers of them appear near the water's surface in what has been called a "frenzied mating dance"—a May worm jubilee.

Nereis is related to its better-known cousin, the bloodworm, which is often used as bait by anglers. The common clamworm is a few inches long, darkly colored with a pulsating artery visible down the middle of its back. It has four eyes, four pairs of tentacles, two fleshy palps, and a retractable proboscis in the head region. The creature inhabits muddy sediments, from the intertidal zone to eelgrass beds to oyster bars. Extruding a mucus it uses to cement sediment into a tube, *Nereis* will capture prey from within this shelter or sometimes emerge to gather macroalgae, animal detritus, or other worms.

In May, these clamworms undergo a metamorphosis into forms specialized for gamete production called heteronereises, and for a few nights on the dark of the moon, they swim to the surface in huge numbers. They swarm, releasing eggs and sperm, and then die. The fertilized eggs soon hatch into planktonic larvae that eventually settle to the bottom of the Bay to assume the mostly sessile life of a clamworm.

Where to see a May worm jubilee this week: Heteronereises are attracted to light, so take a flashlight with you to a dock or pier on a night before the new moon rises. Marshy creeks on the Eastern Shore, such as the Bill Burton Fishing Pier over the Choptank River in Cambridge, are a good bet.

Warbler Migration

Early May is peak warbler migration, when millions of tiny songbirds arrive in our area from the neotropics. On their way to breeding grounds either here or farther north, warblers and other songbirds migrate at night, stopping wherever dawn or nighttime storms overtake them. To most people who are not birders, this dramatic event goes mostly unnoticed; but for naturalists and birders, this is the most exciting, and frenzied, week of the year.

Many bird species that nest in North America spend the colder months in Central America, northern South America, and the Caribbean, where food is more plentiful and environmental conditions less stressful. In contrast, the increased nutritional demands of raising a brood of young require an abundant food source and freedom from the competition of the species-rich tropics. The pulse of insects that appears when trees leaf out provides that extra food, but getting to it requires a migration of hundreds or even thousands of miles. That migration brings its own set of complications and stresses. Still, many species of birds obviously find that twice-yearly journey worthwhile.

Known as neotropical migrants, this cast of characters includes such well-known birds as hummingbirds, orioles, swallows, and thrushes. By far the most numerous are the several dozen species known as wood warblers: small, brightly colored insectivores with distinctive songs. Some warblers arrive in early May and nest here. Among these are yellow warblers, Northern parulas, American redstarts, prothonotary warblers, common yellowthroats, ovenbirds, and Louisiana waterthrushes. Other species are merely passing through on their way to nesting grounds farther north.

Most of these birds, although they weigh only an ounce or two, fly nonstop across the Gulf of Mexico, making landfall on the Gulf Coast in mid-April. After refueling on the abundant insect life there, these feathered pilgrims launch themselves into the sky at dusk, forming virtual rivers of birds in the sky. At dawn, the birds land in suitable habitat and feed voraciously. This is when birding is most profitable and enjoyable, when new discoveries happen every few minutes. At dusk, these birds once again move on, replaced at the next dawn by a new group of migrants. Warbler migration starts in earnest in the last week of April and is mostly over by the end of the second week in May—a short but exciting and wonderful season.

Where to see warblers this week: Good birders seem to be able to find warblers almost anywhere during migration. The key is to be familiar with their songs, then you locate the bird by sound and look with a good pair of binoculars. Most large trees, even on suburban lawns, harbor at least a few warblers this week, but some hotspots reliably yield greater numbers and diversity. These include the C&O Canal towpath, Rock Creek Park, Patuxent Research Refuge, Sugarloaf Mountain, Lake Roland (Robert E. Lee Park), and Susquehanna State Park. On the Eastern Shore, Tuckahoe State Park and Terrapin Nature Park are often productive, as are roads that cross the Pocomoke River and its tributaries. Cape May, New Jersey, is justifiably famous for springtime warblers, and Assateague Island is good for other migrants in addition to warblers.

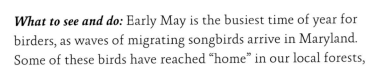

TRIP OF THE WEEK
Second Week of May

Birding for neotropical migrants
Forested areas

What to see and do: Early May is the busiest time of year for birders, as waves of migrating songbirds arrive in Maryland. Some of these birds have reached "home" in our local forests, staking out familiar territories for breeding and nesting. Far greater numbers, however, are only passing through on their way northward. In either case, our forests are filled with singing avian jewels; and since they are here for only a few weeks, pick up your dusty binoculars and do some birdwatching. You don't need to go to any specific place; migrants fill virtually every wooded lot, even in cities. Once you become attuned to migrating birds and their songs, you'll be astonished at how ubiquitous they are. That said, you'll see more birds if you go with a group, where the more experienced participants can advise you about field marks and song patterns that aid in identification. Many local birding groups offer trips, especially at this time of year, and welcome newcomers.

Naturalist's tip: You'll see and hear more birds in the period from first light to perhaps midmorning than any other time of day, because the birds are more active, feeding voraciously after a long night of flying. Good birders listen for the usually distinctive songs, then look for movement in the area where the sound originates, and only then raise binoculars to view the bird, so familiarity with songs and calls is an eminently useful skill. (The Cornell Lab of Ornithology's Macaulay Library [macaulay library.org] contains extensive recordings of birdsong.) If possible, keep the rising sun behind you so the birds are not backlit.

More information: For a list of birding trips around the state, contact the Maryland Ornithological Society (www.mdbirds.org). In addition, the Audubon Naturalist Society offers frequent bird walks in the Washington, D.C. area (www.audubonnaturalist.org).

Blackpoll Warblers,
Last of the Spring Migrants

Blackpoll warblers are not well-known birds, but they are distinctive in several interesting ways. Passing through Maryland mostly on the vernal leg of their twice-yearly migration, blackpolls travel more miles, and more nonstop miles, than any other warbler. Although blackpolls are numerous and vocal while they are here, most Marylanders are not aware of having seen this diminutive songster.

Blackpoll warblers nest in the boreal forests of Alaska and across the entire width of northern Canada. In this remote habitat, they have the highest population density of any warbler species. They overwinter in the forests of South America, especially Brazil. What happens in between is what makes blackpolls interesting.

After raising young in the long, bug-filled summer days of the near-Arctic, blackpolls begin to move south as early as August. Because their migratory path is primarily along the East Coast of the United States, birds from Alaska and western Canada have to cross the continent, several thousand miles of travel, before even starting to move south. They leave New England after one of the first cold fronts of autumn, aided by tailwinds out of the northwest. Migration appears to be over water, because the species is rare in the fall in the southeastern United States but common in the Bahamas and Lesser Antilles. Birds that leave Nova Scotia fly more than 1,000 miles and as much as eighty-eight hours nonstop. While migrating terns and some shorebirds may fly farther, at only about 11 grams, blackpolls are the champions when measured on a weight-to-nonstop-miles ratio. Here in Maryland, we know blackpolls from their spring

Blackpoll warblers are the last neotropical migratory songbird to depart Maryland for more northerly nesting territories. Their distinctive song makes blackpolls a familiar participant in the May morning chorus.

migration. Perhaps less heroically than in the fall trip, some birds apparently island-hop through the Caribbean, while others make longer journeys over water in the company of other warblers. They then move northward from the Gulf Coast over land.

Blackpolls arrive in Maryland usually about the second week in May, our latest-arriving migrant warbler, and they linger through the end of the month. By the third and early in the fourth week of May, blackpolls can be heard regularly in central Maryland, our most common nonresident songbird in this period. Finally, blackpoll warblers seem to be birds of the suburbs, preferring the big, mature oaks in well-established neighborhoods over nearby tracts of unbroken forest.

Blackpoll warblers have a unique and easy-to-identify song.

It is a single note, repeated about twenty times over two to three seconds, loudest in the middle, sounding like a flywheel in need of lubrication. We are fortunate that this distinctive song alerts us to their presence, because blackpolls are hard to see, as they prefer to perch in oak trees, which are fully leafed out by the time the birds arrive in Maryland.

Where to see blackpoll warblers this week: Suburban neighborhoods with scattered big oak trees, like those in Bethesda and Catonsville, are good places to listen for blackpolls' distinctive song.

Multiflora Rose Blooms

Multiflora rose is a shrub with which we humans have a distinctly love-hate relationship. While it is non-native, invasive, and incredibly thorny, multiflora rose flowers emit a wonderful scent that perfumes the landscape, and its fruits are an important autumn food source for wildlife, rich in vitamin C.

Multiflora rose spread rapidly in the 1930s, when planting of it was promoted for erosion control and for wildlife food and cover. It was also planted as a "living fence," to contain livestock and even as a crash barrier on highway median strips. By the 1960s, however, people realized that multiflora rose was replacing and outgrowing native vegetation; its eradication proved difficult. Multiflora rose adapts to a wide variety of habitats and is now common in fallow pastures and forest edges. For better or worse, multiflora rose seems likely to be a part of the Maryland landscape well into the future.

Where to see multiflora rose this week: Multiflora rose is common on disturbed soil in full sun. Look for it under powerline cuts, in your local park, and in the median strips of Interstates 95 and 70.

Carpenter Frogs "Hammering"

Among the cacophony of amphibian calls that split the vernal night over Maryland wetlands, few are as distinctive as that of the carpenter frog. As its name implies, the call sounds exactly like a carpenter hammering nails into wood. While carpenter frogs call day and night and have a long breeding season, mid-May is a likely time to hear them.

In Maryland, carpenter frogs are confined to "Delmarva bays": small, bowl-shaped depressions that hold water year-round and harbor a distinctive flora. Most Delmarva bays are found in remote locations along the Maryland-Delaware border, so carpenter frogs are not common in the Old Line State. The species is far more common in New Jersey's Pine Barrens, where it is associated with wetlands containing sphagnum moss. These bog waters are acidic, and carpenter frogs are quite acid tolerant.

Where to find carpenter frogs this week: Carpenter frogs are sometimes found near the border of Maryland and Delaware, but they are easily heard in sphagnum bogs adjacent to the small rivers of the Pine Barrens of New Jersey.

TRIP OF THE WEEK
Third Week of May
The Pine Barrens
Central southern New Jersey (7 counties)

What to see and do: Occupying more than 100,000 acres of central southern New Jersey, the Pine Barrens is a unique ecoregion harboring unusual plants, scenic rivers, a fascinating human history, and an interesting ecology. Perhaps the best way to experience the Pine Barrens is with a canoe trip down one of its very narrow, twisty, slow-flowing rivers. The Batsto and Mullica are each perfect for an overnight canoe camping trip, while the Wading and Oswego are suitable for a pleasant day trip. There are several outfitters who can provide canoes and shuttles, but try to go on a weekday or in cooler weather, as weekends May through September are very crowded. Hikers will find fifty miles of the Batona Trail crossing the Pine Barrens. The restored mid-nineteenth century Batsto Village with a variety of displays and exhibits is worth a visit.

Naturalist's tip: The Pine Barrens contain many bogs and wet meadows that are home to unusual plants. Look for orchids such as the white fringed orchid and the crested yellow orchid, both flowering in midsummer, and for plants that capture insects, like yellow bladderwort, round-leaved sundew, and pitcher plant.

More information: See www.state.nj.us/dep/parksandforests /parks/wharton.html. Information about the natural history and preservation of the Pine Barrens may be found at www .pinelandsalliance.org.

Diamondback Terrapins Laying Eggs

Turtles rarely make anyone's list of beautiful animals, but the diamondback terrapin, common in Chesapeake Bay, is a handsome and charismatic exception. Its carapace has diamond-shaped concentric ridges on each plate, and the neck and head are gray with wiggly black lines. And as turtles go, diamondback terrapins are fast movers on land, disappearing surprisingly quickly into dense foliage.

Diamondback terrapins are the only turtle that inhabit estuaries where the water is brackish. They have a cosmopolitan diet of clams, crabs, snails, fish, worms, and insects. Even so, terrapins grow slowly; females require seven years to mature, while males take about half that. Mating occurs in early spring, and females trudge ashore in late May to lay eggs in sandy soil. This brief

Female diamondback terrapins are cautious about coming ashore to lay eggs. Once on land, they move quickly to find protected nesting sites.

window is about the only time you are likely to get a good look at a diamondback terrapin, as they are aquatic the rest of the year.

Terrapins hold a special place in Maryland cuisine, at least historically. Terrapin soup was considered a delicacy after the Civil War. An astonishing 89,000 pounds of terrapin were caught in one year in the late 1800s. By the 1920s, overharvesting made terrapins scarce, and since then the soup appears only occasionally on the menus of special gourmet dinners. The reduced population is a far cry from colonial days, when terrapins were so abundant and easily caught that they were the primary source of protein for slaves and indentured servants. Since 2007, it has been illegal to harvest or possess diamondback terrapins in Maryland. Indeed, this handsome animal is the official state reptile.

Where to see diamondback terrapins this week: Terrapins come ashore to lay eggs on many sandy beaches around the perimeter of the lower Chesapeake Bay and on its islands, but they tend to be wary. An exception is on Assateague Island. Check the Bayside campground of Assateague Island National Seashore.

Mountain Laurel Blooming

Mountain laurel may brighten the winter-gray forest with its shiny evergreen leaves, but late May brings this forest shrub into its full and spectacular glory. Clouds of white blossoms cascade over wiry twisted branches, all but obscuring the leaves during this short season of resplendent flowering. Each flower is about an inch across with five fused petals that form a pentagon shape. Bumblebees are the primary pollinator, but mountain laurel can self-fertilize if insects fail to visit. The flower bud is star-shaped and is often pink in color.

Mountain laurel is a member of the heath family, preferring sandy, well-drained dry soil that is often poor in organic matter.

In Maryland, mountain laurel has a wide geographic range, being a common understory shrub in the mountains and forming dense thickets ("laurel hells") on the coastal plain. It can often form pure stands on forested rocky slopes, especially along rivers and creeks. For most of the year, mountain laurel is a modest and unassuming evergreen shrub, but for a few weeks in late spring, its blossoms lend the appearance of a landscape covered by a late snowfall.

Where to see mountain laurel blooming this week: Mountain laurel is a common shrub. Exceptional stands may be found in the campground at the Shad Landing area of Pocomoke River State Park, along the Big Gunpowder River between Prettyboy and Loch Raven Reservoirs, in Rock Creek Park, and along the Appalachian Trail, to name just a few.

Shorebirds and Horseshoe Crabs

The second half of May on the shores of lower Delaware Bay are the time and place of two of the world's great remaining wildlife spectacles: horseshoe crab breeding and shorebird migration. The events are immense in numbers and scale, continental in scope and range, and most Marylanders are blissfully unaware of this awe-inspiring confluence of remarkably disparate yet intimately linked animals. This is a shame, for a late-May day spent at Delaware Bay is not only a vacation from the mundane but a reminder that the natural world goes on without us and in spite of us.

Down at the water's edge, the beach seems to crawl with random movements, like a carpet of distant wildflowers in a breeze or a far horizon shimmering in the heat. Raise your binoculars and witness the source of movement: hordes of tiny shorebirds, shifting and jostling for space, feeding voraciously, as if their time here were a rare and precious commodity. And it is.

The blood of horse-shoe crabs is light blue, because it uses copper, rather than iron, to carry oxygen. Scientists collect amebocytes from the blood of horseshoe crabs and use them to detect bacterial endo-toxins in humans.

They have come from a coastline of South America, having enjoyed the austral summer, and are now moving urgently north to breeding grounds in the Nearctic, where the sun never sets and food is plentiful, for a brief season of mating and nesting and raising young. They include semipalmated sandpiper, red knot, and ruddy turnstone. Even though these birds weigh only a few ounces, they are capable of flying immense distances; but they cannot make it the entire way without a stopover to gorge on some superabundant food source, to recover muscle mass, to restock fat stores, and to prepare for the final push north. That place is a few dozen miles of beach in lower Delaware Bay, and that superabundant food source is the eggs of horseshoe crabs.

Although they also have traveled to get here, the horseshoe crabs have come only from the southern U.S. coast. As the tide rises in Delaware Bay, it brings with it a host of strange-looking armored arthropods, rolling in the surf, singly or in trains or in piles, their spiky, tail-like telsons waving. Chaos rules, pandemonium results, entropy ensues. Dinner-plate-size females lumber ashore, trailed by one or more smaller males, clinging to the females tenaciously, determined to fertilize the eggs of this particular female as she lays them in shallow depressions in the sand. Other crabs, flipped onto their backs by the surf, struggle to right themselves, using their telsons as pry bars. Still others, tossed and stranded by the previous high tide, lie alone, dead or dying, putrefying in the hot spring sun. Millions of tiny green-black eggs mix with the sand and gravel, food for shorebirds. The eggs link these two disparate animals, providing energy and carbon and nutrients that will soon be dispersed to far-off lands of tundra and marsh and ice-choked shoreline.

There is no natural event in the mid-Atlantic area more dramatic, more awe-inspiring, than the union in time and space of shorebirds and horseshoe crabs. All the big themes are present here on the beaches of Delaware Bay. It may look like birds feeding on eggs among crabs, but it's really about struggle and epic journeys and random survival; and ultimately, it's about life and death.

Where to see horseshoe crabs this week: See "Trip of the Week" below.

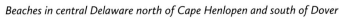

TRIP OF THE WEEK
Fourth Week of May

Delaware Bay to see shorebirds and horseshoe crabs

Beaches in central Delaware north of Cape Henlopen and south of Dover

What to see and do: For a few weeks each year, two of North America's great wildlife migrations meet on the shores of Delaware Bay, as horseshoe crabs arrive from the southern Atlantic coast to breed and lay eggs and shorebirds stop over on their migration from South America to the Arctic to feed on these eggs. Among the locations where there is public access to the beaches are Slaughter Beach, Fowlers Beach, Bowers Beach,

South Bowers Beach, Big Stone Beach, Kitts Hummock Beach, and the road to Port Mahon. In New Jersey, Reeds Beach is a good bet. Be sure to observe all parking and beach access regulations. The best dates are May 15 through 30; by June 1, most of the shorebirds have departed.

Naturalist's tip: The best time to see horseshoe crabs is on the high tide, when they come ashore in greater numbers, and more specifically on the full and new moon, when high tides are higher. Shorebirds are busy all the time, but the receding tide reveals more eggs, and the feeding birds seem more frenzied then.

More information: Visit www.ceoe.udel.edu/horseshoecrab/.

Phalaropes, Polyandry, and Profligacy

The shorebirds rise as one from the beach, their wing-beats a sudden white noise, like distant applause. The flock wheels and turns, beats against the wind for a short while, and then settles to the sand again like a gray snowfall. Hundreds of semipalmated sandpipers, a few ruddy turnstones, and a red knot or two prowl the edge of Delaware Bay, seeking the greenish-black eggs of horseshoe crabs laid carelessly and profligately along the high tide line. I had come to see this, eastern North America's last great wildlife spectacle, but even it had started to lose its charm after a full morning of watching and waiting. I scan the crowd at the water's edge one last time . . . and there it is.

Birders live for the rarities. They may exclaim over trip counts, rhapsodize about a particularly good look at a favorite bird, or watch with fascination an unexpected behavior, but ultimately every birder wants to see a species he or she has never seen before. If the bird is uncommon or unusual, so much the better. My rarity on this day at Port Mahon was a red-necked phalarope.

Phalaropes are pelagic, that is, they come ashore only to breed. Of the three species of phalaropes, the red-necked is the most commonly seen on land. It is spotted more frequently during the fall migration than in spring. Red-necked phalaropes nest on the Arctic tundra and are circumpolar in distribution. Most North American phalaropes winter off the coast of Peru.

This red-necked phalarope was a bit larger than a sandpiper, although from time to time it would be harassed by members of that smaller species and was clearly subordinate to them. It had a white belly and dark back with two reddish-buff stripes. The neck was white, the top of the head black, and a distinctive

Strawberries: False, Wild, and Cultivated

The first week in June is traditionally when strawberries, both wild and cultivated, ripen. It's a short but glorious season of strawberry festivals, homemade strawberry ice cream, and pick-your-own berrying excursions. There are hundreds of varieties of cultivated strawberries, each with its own merits—and problems. Finding a really good cultivated strawberry, one that bursts with flavor and is not too watery or bland, is difficult, even at this time of year. But for the true connoisseur, nothing can match a sun-ripened wild native strawberry, picked from a dew-laden meadow and eaten on the spot. While small and often visually imperfect, these wild strawberries burst with an intense flavor unmatched by any cultivated variety. Wild native strawberries can be uncommon, not easy to locate in the often tick-infested fields they favor, and the vines have often been stripped bare by the many wild animals who enjoy a ripe wild strawberry every bit as much as we humans do. Still, there is no better wild berry, and there is nobility in the search, even if it turns out to be, quite literally, fruitless.

Far more common is the false Indian strawberry, or wood strawberry, a look-alike plant that is often mistaken for its namesake. This common plant of lawns, fields, and trail edges also fruits in the first week in June, although it continues producing yellow flowers and small red fruits throughout the summer. Alas, the fruits are mealy and tasteless, as many an excited child has found, to his or her disappointment.

Where to find strawberries this week: Look for wild strawberries in meadows and power line cuts, wherever vegetation is low and there is plenty of sunlight. False Indian strawberry is common in suburban lawns that are a bit unkempt and untreated with weed killer. The Maryland Department of Agriculture and other sources list farms where you can buy or pick your own culti-vated strawberries.

Sweetbay Magnolias

A small tree of coastal plain swamps, the sweetbay magnolia is easily overlooked until early June, when its large, white, saucer-shaped flowers open. Not just visually attractive, the flowers of this very ancient species release a heavenly scent. These flowers are most easily seen by boat, opening in the full sun where they hang over tidal waters.

Sweetbay magnolias belong to an ancient lineage of flowering plants. Some magnolia species evolved before bees and so are pollinated by beetles.

Where to find sweetbay magnolias this week: The large, white flowers make sweetbay magnolia easy to identify. The small tree is common along the Pocomoke River and its tributaries. For example, paddle a canoe up Corkers Creek in the Shad Landing area of Pocomoke River State Park.

Day Lilies Flowering

By far our most common and widespread lily, day lilies brighten streambanks, shady borders, and even roadside ditches every June. These non-native, invasive plants make a colorful show, even as naturalists curse their penchant for crowding out native vegetation. At least day lilies, both leaf and flower, are eaten by whitetail deer, reducing the effect these voracious herbivores have on native plants. Whitetail deer are not the only mammal to enjoy the taste of day lilies. Humans can pick the orange-tinted blossoms just before they open to make a wonderful, peppery addition to a salad.

Where to see day lilies this week: Day lilies line many rivers and streams in Maryland and have escaped from gardens to populate roadsides and trail edges wherever there is sufficient soil moisture. Among parks where day lilies are common are the C&O Canal National Historical Park, Rock Creek Park, Sugarloaf Mountain, and Gunpowder Falls and Susquehanna State Parks.

Fawns Born

Whitetail deer are the most common large mammal in Maryland, and in mid-May pregnant does give birth to their fawns. Impregnated during the November rut, the does have endured pregnancy throughout the cold winter, when browse is sometimes scarce. The last trimester of the 200-day gestation occurs when the lush new growth of spring provides abundant, nutritious food.

Many whitetails in Maryland give birth to twins, and occa-

Newborn whitetail fawns have little scent. They often remain immobile even when closely approached. Both traits help protect them from predators.

sionally triplets. Adolescent does—they can be impregnated as young as six months—usually bear only a single fawn. Fawns move around infrequently in the first three weeks of life, remaining motionless even when humans walk nearby. After three weeks or so, fawns can keep up with adult deer in running from danger, so early June is when you are most likely to encounter young fawns. This high rate of reproduction and good survivorship rates ensure that whitetails can endure a large hunting harvest each autumn and still populate the Maryland landscape in large numbers.

Where to see whitetail fawns this week: Encountering a young fawn in the wild is unusual, despite the large number of them born about this time each year. However, fawns are seen with some frequency at Big Meadows in Shenandoah National Park (see "Trip of the Week"). Adult deer can reliably be seen in the C&O Canal National Historical Park and Seneca Creek, Patapsco Valley, and many other Maryland state parks, especially in early morning and early evening.

TRIP OF THE WEEK
First Week of June

Shenandoah National Park

82 miles west of Washington, D.C., in Front Royal, Virginia (Warren County), is the northern gateway to this linear park, and Waynesboro, Virginia, is near the southern end.

What to see and do: Poised like a rampart to the southwest of Washington, D.C., Shenandoah National Park is both a refuge and a playground for urbanites who need a close getaway. This linear park, running along the spine of the Blue Ridge, is a slice of wilderness within the human-dominated landscapes of the mid-Atlantic. It is home to black bears, native brook trout, rare plants, and plenty of deer. For those in autos, Skyline Drive reveals vistas both east and west, limited only by haze and air pollution. Miles of hiking trails open up the more remote parts of the park to those willing to walk; the trails lead to waterfalls, mountaintops, and flower-filled meadows. While every part of Shenandoah is wonderful, the central portion is especially scenic. Big Meadows is home to whitetail deer who are unafraid of humans, and black bear are common there after dark. Hawksbill and Stony Man are two of the highest peaks in the park and have impressive views. The handicap accessible Limberlost Trail traverses a virgin hemlock forest, while the nearby Whiteoak Canyon Trail features several waterfalls and cascades.

Naturalist's tip: Early June brings blooming mountain laurel and a diverse assortment of wildflowers at the higher elevations.

More information: Visit www.nps.gov/shen/index.htm.

· WEEK 2 ·

Gypsy Moth Defoliation

A walk in some Maryland oak forests in June can be a surreal experience. The trees, despite the heat of late spring, are bare of leaves; the forest is sunny, lacking a leaf canopy, as though it were a warm day in late March. Stand quietly and you can hear a continual low hum, the sound of thousands of insects munching on the few remaining leaves. All around, a slow rain of leaf fragments and insect frass drifts down, covering every surface. This forest is experiencing an outbreak of gypsy moths, and their larvae are reshaping the ecology of this woods in a way that will persist for years to come.

Unlike with many invasive non-native species, we know exactly when and where gypsy moths first arrived in the United States. In 1869, a Massachusetts scientist imported the insects in a misguided attempt to establish a silk-moth industry here. They soon escaped, and quickly became a pest, defoliating trees throughout New England. Gypsy moths expanded their range slowly southward along the oak-studded ridges of the Appalachians, eventually spreading to all parts of Maryland. The first extensive defoliations occurred in 1981, and for the next two decades, gypsy moths were of significant concern to many Maryland residents. In addition to the unnatural defoliation of trees, many trees died, changing the ecology of forests, woodlots, suburban neighborhoods, and even urban parks. The only good news is that gypsy moth populations usually reach pest proportions only at the leading edge of their range expansion. After the first few years, a pathogenic fungus, *Entomophaga maimaiga*, catches up, often controlling the incidence of gypsy moth damage. However, weather plays a significant role. In dry years, the fungus grows poorly, leading to an outbreak of insects. When *Entomophaga* cannot control gypsy moths, the Maryland

Gypsy moth caterpillars do the most damage to trees at the expanding edge of the insect's geographic distribution. Once established in an area, parasites and predators catch up, reducing the magnitude of gypsy moth outbreaks.

Department of Agriculture sprays afflicted forests with an insecticide. For example, in 2008, the state sprayed more than 100,000 acres of forest, while in 2011, no spraying was needed.

Gypsy moths hatch in April from dun-colored egg masses laid the previous year. The tiny caterpillars crawl to the tops of trees and begin eating leaves and growing. By late May, they are about an inch long, and their cumulative feeding creates noticeable defoliation. Within another few weeks, the larvae have grown to more than two inches long and can chew through a significant volume of leaf material in a day. Gypsy moth caterpillars are easy to identify. They are hairy, dark in color, and have five pairs of blue dots near their anterior end and six pairs of brick-red dots on raised knobs at the posterior. In late June, each larva spins a dark brown teardrop-shaped pupal case, within which the insect completely rearranges its body plan. By early July, the moth emerges from the pupal case. Females do not fly, but males flutter through the forest in search of unmated females. Adult gypsy moths do not feed, and so they die soon after mating and egg deposition.

Maryland forests have been affected by the extensive gypsy moth outbreaks of the 1980s and 1990s. A healthy tree can survive one or even two complete defoliations, but a third is usually fatal. Less healthy trees may succumb to the first or second defoliation. Gypsy moths favor oaks but will eat many other hard-wood tree species. While gypsy moths will remain with us for the foreseeable future, their worst depredations seem to be over.

Where to see gypsy moths this week: If there is a gypsy moth infestation, it will be obvious by the defoliation of trees, but the location of an outbreak cannot be predicted more than a year in advance. For the latest information, see the Maryland Department of Agriculture's site, mda.maryland.gov/plants-pests/pages/gypsy _moth_program.aspx.

Mulberries Ripe

One of the most common wild fruits in our region, mulberries, are now ripe for harvest. The red mulberry, whose fruits are such a deep claret color as to appear almost black, is native to eastern North America. White mulberry, the fruits of which have a much reduced flavor, was brought here from Asia; it has become naturalized, and hybridizes readily with red mulberry. Each berry, actually a cluster of individual drupes, is almost an inch

long and half as wide. The tree itself is unprepossessing until early June, when huge numbers of berries fall to the ground and stain sidewalks, vehicles, or whatever happens to occupy the space beneath its drip line. Red mulberries are sweet and make a nice snack for humans, birds, and animals, free for the taking. Mulberries can also be made into jams, wine, and

Mulberries have a pleasant taste, but their sugar content is not as high as many other fruits.

flavorings; the juice is rich in anthocyanins and resveratrol, both antioxidants.

Common in both urban and suburban neighborhoods as well as in forest and field, mulberry trees are resistant to pollution and drought and tolerate poor soil. A cutting placed in soil quickly grows to a small tree. Red mulberry leaves have a unique shape, with several irregular lobes and a coarsely serrated edge, the upper surface of which feels like sandpaper.

Where to find mulberries this week: Mulberry trees are so common in residential neighborhoods that a short walk will certainly yield one or more berry-laden trees this week. Look for purple stains on concrete or automobiles.

Periodical Cicadas Emerge

While this book is concerned with periodic biological phenomena within the yearly calendar, one regular event is not annual but septendecimal. It is, however, so dramatic that it is worth a mention, even though most of us will experience it fewer than a half-dozen times in our lives. Late spring is when periodical cicadas (incorrectly known as "locusts") emerge, once every seventeen years. Like major hurricanes, cicada years are so memorable that we humans easily recall other events that we associate with that year.

Our seventeen-year cicada is *Magicicada septendecim,* a member of the true bugs, hemipterans, more closely related to aphids than to similarly shaped insects like grasshoppers. Brood X is what emerges in most parts of Maryland, most recently in 2003. The adults are almost two inches long, with red protruding eyes and coarsely veined transparent wings covering most of the body. They fly weakly, often blundering into humans and pets who brave the outdoors during an emergence. However, cicadas neither bite nor sting; they are merely a nuisance.

As noteworthy as their high numbers is the "song" of periodical cicadas. There are actually five songs, all very similar: the alarm call, the calling song (to stimulate assembly of individuals so as to increase loudness), and three slightly different mating calls. Males generate the mating songs, actually a loud buzz, by vibrating an abdominal structure, the tymbal. A group of cicadas singing together may reach one hundred decibels in volume.

Females attracted to these songs mate with a male and then cut V-shaped slits in twigs of deciduous trees, into which they lay small clusters of eggs. The eggs hatch in about six weeks and the tiny nymphs fall to the ground, burrowing downward where they will spend almost two decades siphoning xylem from the roots of trees. After seventeen years underground, the inch-long nymphs emerge, once the soil temperature eight inches down reaches 64°F. Adults do feed during their several-week adult lifespan, sucking sap out of tender twigs. By late June in Maryland, the landscape is quiet again, albeit littered with the carcasses of dead cicadas.

Some small portions of Maryland have periodical cicadas that are on a thirteen-year cycle, and a few areas have seventeen-year cicadas from a different brood, which emerge in a different year from the dominant brood's cycle.

Periodical cicadas have the longest developmental period of any insect. The seventeen-year life cycle is thought to be a response to unpredictably cold summers that occurred during the Pleistocene Epoch; the longer the nymphal life cycle, the smaller the chance of emerging during a cold summer. Predator saturation—huge numbers of cicadas emerging synchronously so as to overwhelm the ability of predators to seriously impact the population—is no longer thought to have driven the evolution of the prime-number-yeared periodicity.

Where to see periodical cicadas this week: For most of Maryland, Brood X cicadas will next emerge in 2020. When that happens, only people who stay within city blocks devoid of trees will be unaware of cicadas. In the meantime, a useful source of information is www.cicadamania.com.

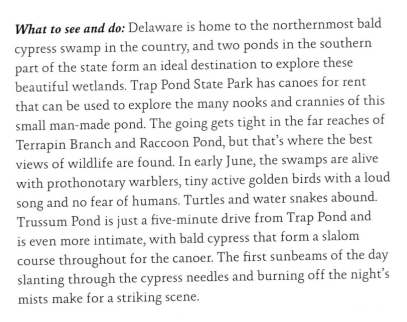

TRIP OF THE WEEK
Second Week in June

Trap Pond State Park and Trussum Pond

6 miles east of Laurel, Delaware (Sussex County)

What to see and do: Delaware is home to the northernmost bald cypress swamp in the country, and two ponds in the southern part of the state form an ideal destination to explore these beautiful wetlands. Trap Pond State Park has canoes for rent that can be used to explore the many nooks and crannies of this small man-made pond. The going gets tight in the far reaches of Terrapin Branch and Raccoon Pond, but that's where the best views of wildlife are found. In early June, the swamps are alive with prothonotary warblers, tiny active golden birds with a loud song and no fear of humans. Turtles and water snakes abound. Trussum Pond is just a five-minute drive from Trap Pond and is even more intimate, with bald cypress that form a slalom course throughout for the canoer. The first sunbeams of the day slanting through the cypress needles and burning off the night's mists make for a striking scene.

Naturalist's tip: If you own your own canoe and water levels permit, and if downed trees have been cleared out, the James Branch Water Trail from Trap Pond downstream to Records Pond is superb swamp cruising on a stream barely wider than the canoe. Few people have paddled this little stream, which harbors the largest bald cypress trees in Delaware.

More information: Visit www.destateparks.com/park/trap-pond /index.asp.

Mockingbirds Singing

The longest days of the year wake most humans earlier than usual, but the champion early riser at this season is that common bird of both town and country, the northern mockingbird. For much of June, male mockingbirds often sing all night long. Seemingly indefatigable, mockers provide us with a melodic reminder that the breeding season is under way. Most birds try to keep a low profile when their young are fledging, but the aggressive mockingbird relies on a pugnacious nature and conspicuous aural displays to warn off predators.

Northern mockingbirds are adept mimics, singing the songs of dozens of other bird species.

Mockingbirds can learn as many as 200 different songs, and a favorite pastime of good birders is to see how many songs of other bird species they can recognize when a mockingbird is holding forth. But mockingbirds don't just imitate other birds; they have been heard to reproduce sirens, car alarms, and barking dogs. There is even a documented case of a mockingbird who lived in a military cemetery singing some of the notes from "Taps"! Males with the largest repertoire generally have the best territories and leave the most offspring; learning ability correlates with fitness.

Where to see mockingbirds this week: Mockingbirds nest throughout all of Maryland except parts of Garrett County. They are plentiful and are visually and vocally conspicuous. Any suburban neighborhood will yield a flash of white wing bars, a flipping tail, and the cheerfully varied song of a mockingbird.

Sea Nettles Appear in the Bay

Chesapeake Bay is a wonderful recreational resource, but much of the mid-Bay is not suitable for swimming due to sea nettles. These primitive but successful members of the jellyfish family often appear by mid-June, just a few weeks after the water warms sufficiently for swimming. Only in persistently wet years, when freshwater inflow keeps salinities low, will the Bay remain nettle-free. *Chrysaora quinquecirrha* is truly an estuarine creature. It will not grow if the salinity is less than 7 parts per thousand or greater than 25 (ocean water is usually about 33 parts per thousand). Sea nettles thus avoid many of the predators and competitors that control the more oceanic species of jellyfish.

The life cycle of sea nettles is annual. Adults release either eggs or sperm (the sexes are separate) into the water in prodigious amounts sometime around July. One large female can release 40,000 eggs *daily* for much of the summer! After fertilization, the larvae attach to hard surfaces and grow into vase-like polyps. These polyps overwinter and form young sea nettles as waters warm in late spring. Sea nettles eat primarily copepods and other zooplankton, as well as comb jellies, small fish, and fish larvae.

Where to see sea nettles this week: Sea nettles are hard to avoid mid-Bay unless there has been a wet spring. They are usually abundant in the Wye River, most often accessed via Wye Landing.

Self-heal Flowering

Sometimes we fail to appreciate the commonplace, and this little herb of lawn and garden, forest and field, falls into that category. It's hard to spend a day outdoors without encountering *Prunella vulgaris*, as its Latin specific name implies. The small but beautiful hooded flowers, blue to light purple in color, often form a symmetrical pattern when viewed from above. Self-heal is a member of the mint family, so it has a square stem, but there is no discernible scent. This familiar plant has been used in herbal medicine, as treatment for a variety of ailments. One colorful recipe calls for placing a teaspoon of the dried flowerheads into a pint of good rye whiskey and taking as

In the wild, self-heal grows up to a foot in height, but in frequently mowed lawns, they may be only an inch tall.

needed. Such a concoction is guaranteed to have a physiological effect, but which is the active ingredient may be a bit unclear. Self-heal is in flower from now until frost, but the most vigorous plant growth is in mid-June. It adapts to mowing by staying short; such plants may be only an inch high, but they still form prolific flowers.

Where to find self-heal this week: Look for this plant anywhere weeds grow, including untended lawns and the edges of trails.

It is common in parks such as Gunpowder Falls and Patapsco Valley State Parks, as well as Rock Creek Park.

Rhododendrons in Bloom

River banks in western Maryland often exhibit a solid wall of dense shrubs that are now flowering in beautiful clusters of white or pale pink blooms. Rosebay rhododendron is very common and occupies the Appalachian mountains from Georgia to New England. A robust shrub with large, thick, deep green, waxy leaves, rhododendron prefers well-drained acidic soils like those under hemlock trees. Its roots often grow around rocks and boulders in search of purchase and nutrients along the edges of whitewater rivers like the Youghiogheny. Rhododendron grows slowly, since light is dim in such forested situations, but the plant can form thick tangles where more light reaches its leaves. Rhododendron is similar in appearance to mountain laurel, but has larger leaves and flowers. The shrub grows mostly vegetatively via sprouts from the trunk.

Where to see rhododendrons in flower this week: The banks of the Youghiogheny River as it flows through Swallow Falls State Park and Ohiopyle State Park are lined with beautiful rhododendrons, as are most rivers and creeks on the Appalachian Plateau.

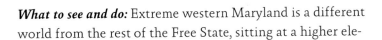

TRIP OF THE WEEK
Third Week of June

Swallow Falls State Park and Cranesville Bog
8 miles north of Oakland (Garrett County)

What to see and do: Extreme western Maryland is a different world from the rest of the Free State, sitting at a higher elevation, with longer winters and cooler summers. Rivers flow not into Chesapeake Bay but west to the Monongahela, the Ohio, and the Mississippi Rivers. Swallow Falls State Park and Cranesville Bog are perhaps the two most scenic and interesting destinations on Maryland's Appalachian Plateau.

Swallow Falls is a small state park that packs a lot of scenery into its 257 acres. The Youghiogheny River (pronounced "yock-i-gay-nee") tumbles over the park's namesake waterfall and then continues boiling steeply downstream over ledges and around boulders in dramatic rapids. The river is lined with native wild rhododendrons that bloom in large snowy clusters this week. Adjacent to the river is a forty-acre virgin hemlock forest. The huge trees tower more than a hundred feet overhead and cast a deep shade on the spongy forest floor, which is carpeted with conifer needles that have accumulated over decades.

Less than five miles from Swallow Falls is Cranesville Bog, owned by the Nature Conservancy. This is a "frost pocket" bog, a wetland containing a variety of unique plants and animals more typical of Canada than Maryland. Cranberry and round-leaved sundews are in flower now. Look also for tamarack, sphagnum moss, alder flycatchers, Nashville warblers, snowshoe hares, and northern water shrews.

Naturalist's tip: The Canyon Trail, paralleling the Youghiogheny River in Swallow Falls State Park, features overhanging slabs of sandstone. There are fossilized tree trunks visible in some of these rocks. Vertical cliffs harbor rock tripe, lichens that in colonial times were used to make a crude soup that was starvation fare.

More information: To learn about Swallow Falls, visit www.dnr .state.md.us/publiclands/western/swallowfalls.asp. For information about Cranesville Bog, go to www.nature.org/ourinitiatives /regions/northamerica/unitedstates/westvirginia/placeswepro tect/cranesville-swamp-preserve.xml.

Enchanter's Nightshade

The summer solstice brings this diminutive and easily-overlooked woodland plant into flower. Despite its unassuming nature, enchanter's nightshade competes favorably with other wildflowers for the title of most evocative name.

Enchanter's nightshade is a member of the genus *Circaea*, named for the Greek goddess Circe. Circe was well known for her magical spells and potions. Supposedly, she used another species in this genus for such purposes, hence the word "enchanter's." The leaves of this species resemble leaves of the nightshade family, providing the rest of its common name. It is not in the nightshade family, however, and to my knowledge has not been used as a medicine or food.

Enchanter's nightshade grows on the forest floor in rich, slightly damp, well-shaded soil. The white flowers are tiny, less than a quarter inch in diameter, and grow on spikes (racemes) that rise above the egg-shaped leaves. The flowers have only two petals, an unusual characteristic shared by only one other genus of native wildflowers, the spurges. It's worth a close look, even though few hikers even notice this modest plant.

Where to see enchanter's nightshade this week: Because it is easily overlooked, few people know enchanter's nightshade. Look for it trailside in places such as Patapsco Valley and Seneca Creek State Parks, Rock Creek Park, and Sugarloaf Mountain.

Blueberries Ripe

The long days of late June ripen blueberries, and long distance hikers on the Appalachian Trail in Maryland appreciate this tasty supplement to their spartan diets. Blueberries are a common ground cover on sandy, nutrient-poor soils, whether they be on mountaintop ridges in the western part of the state or in pine-dominated forests on the coastal plain of the Eastern Shore. These are not the lush commercial berries you buy at the supermarket. Wild blueberries in this region are pea-sized and more tart than sweet.

Where to find wild blueberries this week: Blueberries grow in many places in Maryland where there is dry soil. The Appalachian Trail has many miles of such ridgetop habitat.

Fireflies Light Up the Night

What is more magical than the glow of fireflies in the gloaming? Generations of kids have chased, captured, and observed these commonplace beetles and in the process become familiar, even enchanted, with the natural world. Fireflies don't require wilderness. The suburban lawn seems to host very high densities of these animals with flashing lights on their abdomens. Although the first fireflies may appear by Memorial Day and persist well into July, late June seems to be the high point of their activity.

Where to see fireflies this week: Most suburban lawns host fireflies; you can even see some in grassy areas in cities. Densities seem greatest at the border between forest and lawn.

Brown Pelicans Raising Young

No natural place in Maryland may be more chaotic, noisy, and smelly than a nesting colony of brown pelicans. When adult birds arrive with fish to feed their young, the excited and raucous cries of these nestlings fill the air. Conditions in a colony are often crowded, and territorial squabbles are frequent. The smells of regurgitated fish, bird guano, and the occasional dead bird, all baking in the mid-summer sun, are pungent. A visit to a seabird nesting colony is a memorable experience.

In the Chesapeake, our largest colonial nesting waterbird is the brown pelican. With a six-foot wingspan, few birds are

Brown pelicans have only recently expanded their range northward into Maryland.

more conspicuous and familiar to Maryland beachgoers. Most often seen as a line of birds cruising seemingly without effort just above the waves, these handsome birds are also notorious panhandlers dockside. Less often are pelicans seen feeding, but their headfirst plunge-dive into the ocean in search of fish is a dramatic sight.

Brown pelicans are fairly new to Maryland. Their numbers in the United States were decimated by organochlorine pesticides in the 1960s; the species was once even extinct in Louisiana, where it was (and is) the state bird. After DDT was banned in the United States, brown pelicans made an amazingly rapid recovery, reaching historic levels by 2000. As the population grew, birds on the Atlantic coast expanded their range northward above North Carolina, nesting for the first time in Maryland waters in 1987. In 2010, about 2,500 brown pelican chicks were banded on Bay islands near the Virginia border. By late summer, pelicans are a common sight at Ocean City, Maryland, and are now seen as far north as New Jersey.

Where to see nesting brown pelicans this week: While pelicans in flight and fishing in Maryland are easy to spot, nesting birds are found mostly on uninhabited islands in Chesapeake Bay. As of this writing, the largest colony is on Holland Island, but that will doubtless change, as Holland is being steadily eroded away. Nesting waterbirds are very susceptible to disturbance by humans, with very negative results, so observe the colonies with binoculars from a boat at least fifty feet offshore. Never go ashore; some birds would very likely die due to such an intrusion.

Chesapeake Bay islands

Crisfield (Somerset County) is where ferries to Smith and Tangier Islands depart. Crisfield is 31 miles south of Salisbury (Wicomico County)

What to see and do: A world apart. That's how best to describe Smith Island, Maryland, and Tangier Island, Virginia. Residents of these two islands, many of whose families have lived there for generations, make a living off the waters of Chesapeake Bay and are closely attuned to its cycles. Nature is literally everywhere you look, and sunsets are often unparalleled. Life proceeds at a slower pace. Each island has a small number of accommodations for visitors from the mainland. Access is by boat; Crisfield, Maryland, services both islands daily. Reservations for the ferry and for accommodation are a must. For a unique getaway not to be missed by anyone enchanted with the Chesapeake Bay, spend a day or two on Smith or Tangier Island.

Naturalist's tip: Rent a kayak and paddle the Smith Island Water Trail to experience the marshes that surround the island and to see its wildlife.

More information: Visit www.smithisland.org or www.tangier island-va.com.

A Journey down a Swampy River

Toting our canoe, we wend our way along the narrow path that follows the river downstream from the road bridge. We dance along, dodging the poison ivy and stinging nettles, swatting the stray mosquito, and avoiding stepping on the dainty little violets blooming modestly trailside, until we reach the sandbar at the elbow in the creek where the current gathers itself and rushes noisily over shallow gravels. It'll go; the stream has water enough to get a canoe down without scraping, although the obstacle course of sodden logs and branches that lies just downstream may require some portaging. The sun is shining on this early June morning, a few "godbeams" dapple the fast-disappearing morning mists, and birdsong echoes through the cathedral of leafy boughs arching over the river. It is a morning when all creation seems new, or at least refreshed, and so we are eager to slide our canoes into the current, dip our paddles into the tea-colored water, and see what lies around the next bend.

Tuckahoe Creek is an intimate little stream flowing through the agricultural flatlands of Caroline and Queen Anne Counties on its way to tidewater. For much of its length, a thin ribbon of forest and swamp borders the river, a line of green so narrow on maps that it might easily be written off as having no significant value or interest. But from the woven-cane seat of a canoe, the Tuckahoe seems much larger than it really is, and with its edging of swamp and forest it forms a refuge isolated from the busyness of humankind and a haven for the many animals that have nowhere else to live in this intensively farmed landscape.

The Tuckahoe is as magical as we hoped it would be. The flow is languid but steady, with just enough force that a well-placed paddle stroke will spin the canoe around a stump or over a sunken branch. Where the current runs against the smooth, wet-packed clay of the river bank, mountain laurel blossoms form a snowy, pink-tinged cloud overhanging the creek. The pebble-sized gravels of cobble bars appear cemented together with dark green, almost blackish algae that gather the sparse sunlight, and freshwater clams the size of oysters are wedged in between the cobbles. Always, always there is the sound of bird-song, dozens of species of warblers and vireos, flycatchers and woodpeckers, wrens and thrushes, singing exuberantly in this season of breeding and nesting and raising young.

Rounding a bend, we see a downed tree spanning the creek, but it is easily limboed under. Soon there is another, sheathed in poison ivy, requiring a short carry through the swamp. A third log is partly submerged, and we almost but not quite make it over, hanging up amidships, the hull teetering like a seesaw. I climb out of the canoe into thigh-deep water, clear but tannin-stained, to haul the canoe over the log. From a small limb a few feet away, a tiny golden-headed bird lets loose a string of avian invective, a loud series of *tsip* notes, as he hops back and forth, clearly agitated at this intrusion on his territory. Obviously, this is one brave bird, unconcerned about my size relative to his, full of chutzpah, a living creature in which the fire of life burns bright. A prothonotary warbler.

I admire this beautiful bird from just a few feet away, enchanted by such an intimate encounter, but only slowly do I realize that the reason for this verbal assault is a nest cavity in the downed tree to my right. Prothonotaries are our only warbler species that nest in tree cavities, and this male is doing his best to lead me away from his new family.

Prothonotary warblers spend our winter in the mangrove swamps of central and northern South America. By April they are moving north, and typically they arrive in Maryland in the last week of April or early in the first week of May. Immediately, males begin staking out territories, singing vigorously from perches at the borders, and chasing trespassing neighbors. As prothonotaries dash across the river, they seem to pay no attention to people. I have felt air from their wings brush by my bare shoulder, and there is a report in the literature of a prothonotary perching atop the head of a researcher. Even now, a few weeks later, prothonotaries are still singing vigorously, and we are almost never out of earshot of them for the rest of our trip.

The river unfurls its secrets only when our progress downstream slows. Paddling silently through a marshy sunlit stretch, a splash breaks the quiet, and I glimpse movement of a sleek brown body entering the water. Otter? Beaver? Muskrat? We ship our paddles, letting the current carry us along, scarcely daring to breathe. There, lying on the river bottom, staring up at us, is a beaver, its spatula-shaped tail unmistakable. For a moment, our eyes meet. I see no fear, only curiosity, from this animal so adapted to its watery environment and here so rarely disturbed by humans that it seems totally at peace, unalarmed by our intrusion, unconcerned by our presence, even here on its home territory.

But the creek's flow is inexorable, carrying us seaward, and the few seconds of magic pass. Certainly these animals—beaver and prothonotary warbler—will have forgotten us by day's end, but for us the memory persists, an instant when we were allowed a brief glimpse into the world of wild creatures living in harmony with their world.

July

· WEEK 1 ·

Least Terns Fledging

The smallest of our several species of terns, least terns are fast, nimble fliers. Historically, least terns have nested on Atlantic coastal and Chesapeake Bay beaches and on sand and gravel bars of inland rivers. They are unusual in that, as their beach nesting habitat has disappeared, they have taken to setting up housekeeping on flat, gravel-covered roofs of schools, malls, and similar buildings. They were first observed nesting on rooftops in 1951; in the 1990s, students in several eastern Baltimore County schools monitored nesting colonies atop their school buildings. In changing their nesting behavior, these beautiful shorebirds have demonstrated an adaptive flexibility that has enabled them to survive nearly critical decreases in population sizes.

Least terns arrive in the Chesapeake in early May and soon pair off. The male offers a fish to his intended, and if it is accepted, mating occurs. Eggs are laid in a simple scrape nest a few days later and then incubated for about three weeks. Upon hatching, least terns in rooftop nests face at least two problems not faced by nestlings in natural sites. First, rooftops are

Least terns sometimes nest on flat-roofed buildings now that many of their historic beach nesting sites have been lost to development.

hotter than beaches. The tar on which gravel is overlaid sometimes oozes through, burning the terns' feet and contaminating their developing feathers. Young terns often solve this problem by congregating in the shadow of air conditioners and parapets. Second, some buildings lack parapets, and the free-roaming chicks can tumble to the ground below. Students monitoring colonies of terns have helped by setting up chicken wire fencing on such rooftops. Despite these problems with rooftop nesting, these terns have one advantage over their beach-nesting brethren: minimal predation. No raccoons or foxes can reach these roofs, and aerial predators like gulls and owls are less likely to find these unusual locations far from water.

In early July, young terns are getting their feathers and learning to fly. Once they can fly, they stay with and are fed by their parents until fully independent. By late August, both generations are off to their winter beaches in Central and South America, leaving our skies empty of calling, diving terns until the next spring.

Where to see least terns this week: Just because you see least terns one day at a certain location is no guarantee you'll see them there the next. Look for them near flat-roofed buildings close to the Bay. Chesapeake and Sparrows Point High Schools have hosted colonies. Beaches like those on Hart-Miller and Poplar Islands and at Sandy Point State Park and Chesapeake Bay Environmental Center are also likely places to see least terns.

Annual Cicadas Singing

Each year, the arrival of consistently hot weather in Maryland is accompanied by the distinctive song of annual cicadas, sometimes called "dog day cicadas." These cicadas emerge every year, unlike the incorrectly named "seventeen-year locusts." Annual cicadas are about two inches long with bulging, wide-set eyes and transparent, veined wings held tent-like over the body. They are present for about six weeks each summer.

The "song" of a cicada is species specific and quite loud, up to 120 decibels when measured at close range; it has been described as resembling a power saw cutting wood. The sound is caused by "timbals," a pair of stiff membranes found on the lower abdomen. Muscles cause the membranes to flex in and out, creating a click, up to 400 times a second. Made only by males, the dog day cicada's song is designed to attract females.

After mating, the female uses her ovipositor to cut a slit in a handy twig and then deposits her eggs in the slit. After about six weeks, the eggs hatch and the young nymphs fall to the ground. They burrow underground, and for the next three years or so they feed on the root sap of trees. The final nymphal instar digs to the surface, emerges at night, climbs a nearby plant, and molts to form the winged adult. Thus, more than 95 percent of the life of an annual cicada is spent underground.

Cicadas are big and tasty treats for common predators such as Swainson's hawks and cicada killer wasps.

Where to find annual cicadas this week: Cicadas are so common that, after the first few, we hardly notice their sound, despite how loud it is. It is part of our summer sound track. Any neighborhood with large trees, like Towson or Silver Spring, will have annual cicadas. While hearing cicadas is easy, seeing them is more difficult, since they are arboreal, but occasionally an injured insect will be found on the ground.

Queen Anne's Lace in Flower

This conspicuous flower of grassy fields is common and well known. Queen Anne's lace is a biennial; in the first year it is prostrate, with fernlike, deeply dissected leaves that smell strongly of carrot when crushed. Indeed, its Latin binomial is *Daucus carota*; our familiar garden carrot and Queen Anne's lace are merely different subspecies. The leaves are most noticeable in late fall and early spring, when they are often still green among mostly brown vegetation. In the second year, the plant grows about three feet in height and is topped by a flat, circular cluster of white flowers called an umbel. While each individual flower is tiny, the entire cluster is about three inches across. Only the central flower is red and serves to attract insects. Later in the season, the umbel curls up, and may be mistaken for a bird's nest. Old herbals state that a teaspoon of Queen Anne's lace seeds is useful in preventing pregnancy, although the evidence is anecdotal and contradictory.

Where to see Queen Anne's lace this week: This wild carrot is common in unmowed fields and lots and along roadsides. Reliable sites include the Beltsville Agricultural Research Center, Patuxent Wildlife Research Center, and Gettysburg National Military Park.

TRIP OF THE WEEK
First Week of July

Gettysburg National Military Park
Surrounding Gettysburg, Pennsylvania (Adams County)

What to see and do: Perhaps the most significant battle in American history took place during the first three days of July 1863, at Gettysburg, Pennsylvania, just a few miles north of central Maryland. The large battlefield has been faithfully restored and maintained, and the National Park Service offers the opportunity to learn as much about the battle as you wish. To visit in early July and experience the heat and humidity as the soldiers did 150 years ago (except they were wearing heavy, often wool uniforms) heightens one's appreciation of their valor and dedication to duty. While the battlefield can be toured by auto, perhaps the ideal way to explore the park is by bicycle, where it is a simple matter to dismount to view monuments, explore rarely visited byways, and enjoy fresh air and the sounds of nature. The Gettysburg battlefield is a strikingly attractive rolling landscape of forest and field that is well worth a visit for its natural features, in addition to its great historical significance.

Naturalist's tip: For years, whitetail deer were protected from hunting in the Gettysburg Park, but they reached a high population density and overgrazed delicate forest vegetation. Finally, when their browsing changed the appearance of the park from what it was in 1863, Park Service officials greatly reduced the herd size. The vegetation responded. Wildflowers soon repopulated the forest floor, tree seedlings began to grow to the sapling stage, and as a result the park now has a more natural appearance.

More information: Visit the National Park Service at www.nps.gov/gett/index.htm.

• WEEK 2 •

Early Birds of Autumn

The summer solstice has just passed, but for some animals, autumn has begun. Locally, killdeer and swallows are flocking; the nesting season is over and fledglings now are on their own. Swallows are not yet ready to move south, but they know the day is coming. More conspicuously, several shorebird species are arriving here in Maryland in small but consistent numbers, fresh from their Arctic breeding grounds. Among them are "peeps," the nickname given the five smallest species of sandpiper. It takes a good birder and fine binoculars or a spotting scope to tell one sandpiper species from another, but "peeps" can be distinguished from others if you look very carefully.

The earliest arrival is the least sandpiper, only about six inches long from bill to tail. Leasts nest on sub-Arctic tundra across much of North America in early to mid-May, eschewing the late May feast on Delaware Bay horseshoe crab eggs upon which other shorebirds depend. Incubation takes about twenty days and the precocial chicks learn to fly two weeks after hatching. Almost immediately after that, the parents head south, females preceding males by a few days. The young of that year and late breeders follow a bit later. While most least sandpipers fly nonstop from the Gulf of St. Lawrence to northeast South America, some meander southward in a more leisurely fashion, and it is these birds whom we see on Bay and Atlantic beaches by the second and third weeks in July.

Where to see early birds of autumn this week: Atlantic beaches on Assateague Island and Chesapeake Bay beaches like those of Hart-Miller and Poplar Island are good bets for these shorebirds and other early fall migrants.

Lyme Disease

July is the month when most cases of Lyme disease are reported; June runs a close second. This means that transmission of this tick-borne disease most likely occurred during the month of May.

Lyme disease is caused by the bacterium *Borrelia burgdorferi,* which is transmitted to humans through the bite of an infected deer tick. Of the two common ticks in our area, deer ticks are generally dark, while dog ticks have a cream-colored mantle over the thorax region. The nymphal stage of the deer tick is more likely than the adult to cause disease transfer. It is smaller than a sesame seed and is rarely noticed. In most cases, the tick must be attached for at least twenty-four hours before transmission occurs. Embedded ticks of any species should be removed with fine tweezers. Trying to get the tick to back out by smothering the area in petroleum jelly or by touching the tick with a still-hot, extinguished match does not work.

About 80 percent of patients with Lyme disease develop a distinctive "bulls-eye" rash at the bite site, which develops within one to two weeks. The rash is accompanied, or soon followed by, other symptoms, which may include fatigue, fever, muscle and joint aches, chills, and swollen lymph nodes. Should you have any of these or other odd symptoms and have been bitten by a tick, be sure to tell your doctor, as Lyme disease is occasionally undiagnosed, especially in those patients without the rash. A course of antibiotics will readily cure the disease if given early enough, but severe long-term complications may result if diagnosis is delayed. The disease is less amenable to antibiotics once the bacterium has become latent in the body.

Colorful Wildflowers of Road and Sidewalk Edges

This week finds two species of wildflowers blooming conspicuously near roads and sidewalks: mullein and chicory. Both have long flowering seasons, so you'll find them through much of the summer.

Mullein. Notable for its tall (up to six feet) flower stalk, mullein looks much like a flaming candle. Indeed, colonists dipped the flower stalk in wax or tallow to form torches. Each individual flower is small—less than an inch across—and lasts only a day, but given their great number, their long blooming season, and the size of the flower stalk, they remain a showy plant for

many weeks. Mullein is prolific. More than 100,000 seeds per plant is not unusual, and the seeds can persist in the soil seed bank for a century. For this reason, mullein is an early colonizer of barren or recently burned ground. It is a poor competitor, however, and is quickly displaced by other species.

Mullein is a biennial plant, taking two seasons to complete its life cycle. In

The tall flower stalks of mullein were once dipped in tallow and used as torches. Mullein produces prodigious quantities of seeds, which germinate and grow best on barren ground where there is little competition.

the first year, the plant puts out wooly, silvery-green, velvet-like leaves. This gives the plant its amusing folk name of "cowboy toilet paper." More locally, the leaves were pinned inside clothing to collect body odors. The leaves were also smoked for problems of the throat and lungs. In the second year the tall flower stalk appears and grows, making the plant far more conspicuous.

Chicory. Another plant of edge habitat, particularly sidewalks, is chicory. Like mullein, chicory is a native of Europe but has grown here since early colonial days and is fully naturalized. The plant, which grows one to three feet tall, is a perennial with a deep taproot that makes it hard to eradicate. Chicory is easily identified by its sky-blue, dandelion-like flowers. Each flower opens at dawn and often closes by late afternoon, lasting

Chicory is a tough plant, often found growing out of cracks in sidewalks. The sky-blue flowers persist from late spring through frost.

but a day. Leaves are sparse, giving the stem a bare appearance. Chicory is actually a useful and beneficial plant. Where it grows in pastures, it is readily eaten by cattle and sheep. This helps livestock, as chicory contains a chemical that is toxic to intestinal parasites. It is perhaps more commonly known that the roots of chicory can be used as a coffee-like substitute when baked and ground.

These two common plants of summer share several attributes: they are prolific, conspicuous, originally native to Europe but now naturalized, and bloom for months. They brighten the margins of our highways and sidewalks, and our lives.

Where to see mullein and chicory this week: Look for the distinctive flower stalk of mullein on any disturbed ground, such as abandoned railroad rights-of-way, steep rocky slopes, and along the shoulders of roads and highways. Interstate 70 in Frederick County seems to have more than its fair share of conspicuous mullein plants. Chicory is one of only a few plants that grows well in cracks in sidewalks, so you can find them even in urban situations, in empty lots and beside sidewalks in Baltimore and certainly along the Rock Creek Trail in Washington, D.C.

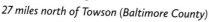

TRIP OF THE WEEK
Second Week of July
Hemlock Gorge
27 miles north of Towson (Baltimore County)

What to see and do: The deep shade of hemlock trees overhanging this narrow gorge of the Gunpowder River makes for a cool haven from the heat of summer. Located in extreme northwestern Baltimore County, Hemlock Gorge is not well known and not easy to get to, but is well worth a visit. The water is cold and clear, and there are several good swimming holes. Large boulders covered in moss and algae lend a shaggy and damp sensibility to the river valley. The occasional beam of sunlight sometimes makes it through the dense hemlock branches, briefly illuminating the river like a spotlight, and early morning mists can make a dramatic scene. An unmarked narrow trail that in places is slippery and requires rock scrambling, parallels the river, which ends at the backwaters of Prettyboy Reservoir. Hemlock Gorge itself is only about a third of a mile long, but it packs some photogenic scenery into such a short distance.

Naturalist's tip: There are still virgin hemlocks in Hemlock Gorge, remnants of precolonial times. A few of these trees are several feet in diameter. However, their existence is threatened by the wooly adelgid, an insect that sucks phloem from young twigs of hemlock trees. Unfortunately, mortality is high in severely infected hemlocks.

More information: See *Baltimore Trails,* by Bryan MacKay (Baltimore: Johns Hopkins University Press, 2008).

Cicada Killer Wasps on Patrol

In late July, giant wasps appear near raised flower beds and sparse lawns, terrifying most people who don't know about cicada killers. Although they look and act fearsome, these beautiful wasps are generally harmless to people, and while males often engage in acrobatic chases of one another, the males cannot sting.

Cicada killer wasps have a similar coloration to yellow jackets but are much larger—up to one and a half inches long—and are quite robust. Adults emerge from underground burrows in loose, dry soil. The males emerge one to two weeks before females. Male cicada killers are very territorial and aggressive toward other males. When virgin females emerge, they are quickly mated by the first available male, although "scrums" of several competing males sometime occur.

While the adult male eats flower nectar and tree sap, the female searches for cicadas. Stinging her prey (females can sting humans but rarely do), the cicada is flown or dragged to a burrow. Here, the female wasp lays a single egg inside the cicada and walls it off in a cell. The number of cicadas the female cicada killer deposits in the cell determines the sex of her offspring. If the egg gets one cicada, it will develop into a male, while eggs with two or three cicadas in the cell develop into females. The egg hatches in two to four days and feeds off the body of the cicada(s) for four to ten days more. It then spins a cocoon and overwinters in the burrow. Adult cicada killers live for only about a month.

Where to see cicada killers this week: Cicada killer wasps tend to be found in raised flower beds and areas of disturbed soil that have been pesticide-free for many years. Cromwell Valley Park in Baltimore County is one such location.

Black-eyed Susans in Bloom

The Maryland State Flower (officially, our "floral emblem") is perhaps our best-known and best-loved wildflower of deep summer. A sun-loving plant, black-eyed susans do well in fields, along roadsides, and in gardens, in poor or rich soil, and regardless of whether the summer has been wet or dry. These lovely plants are annuals or short-lived perennials, but they produce seed in such quantity that they seem present every year. Black-eyed susans spread readily and are common to most of North America.

Black-eyed susans, the Maryland state flower, are familiar wildflowers of garden and field.

Black-eyed susans have composite flower heads with bright yellow "petals" and a chocolate to deep purple central disk. What appear to be petals actually are complete flowers, called ray flowers, with tiny reproductive structures present at the base of each. The central disk contains hundreds of very small flower buds organized in a tightly packed whorl. A close look will reveal that each day a few of the buds will bloom as tiny perfect yellow disk flowers, so small that they appear like yellow pollen atop the dark-colored disk.

Where to see black-eyed susans this week: Cultivated black-eyed susans are common in flower beds and on highway median strips where they have been planted. Power line right-of-ways, like those between Baltimore and Washington, D.C, often host the wild variety of black-eyed susans.

Hottest Days of the Year

We tend to think of the "dog days" of early August as being the most uncomfortably hot days of the year, but meteorological records indicate otherwise. The period July 16-25 holds that unenviable record. During these days, the average high is 88°F, while the average low is 66°F. While those are the statistics, we who have lived a long time in Maryland would swear that every day in late July bakes in 90-something-degree temperatures with high humidity and that a night below 70 would be an unheard-of blessing. The only relief in sight is that the days are getting noticeably shorter, with the accompanying promise of cooler weather.

TRIP OF THE WEEK
Third Week of July

Harpers Ferry, West Virginia, for history and tubing

21 miles southwest of Frederick (Frederick County)

What to see and do: Located at the spectacular confluence of the Potomac and Shenandoah Rivers, Harpers Ferry, West Virginia, is a scenic treasure rich with human and natural history. Much of the lower town has been restored by the National Park Service to the way it looked in 1859, and the fascinating museums, displays, and living history enactments are well worth a visit at any time of year. In the heat of midsummer, an enjoyable way to experience the mountain scenery is by tubing down either of the two rivers. Both rivers include lots of easy rapids to bounce and float through, and the water will keep you cool on even the hottest day. It's an exhilarating yet relaxing way to experience a river from the perspective of a river otter or Canada goose.

Naturalist's tip: The big silver maples lining the Potomac River near Harpers Ferry harbor plentiful numbers of nesting Baltimore orioles in May through August. Prothonotary warblers, small active golden birds, nest in tree cavities along the C&O Canal; the Harpers Ferry area marks the northwestern edge of the range where they are commonly found in Maryland. The C&O Canal towpath hosts a diverse assemblage of wildflowers throughout the growing season.

More information: To learn more about the historical exhibits of Harpers Ferry, visit www.nps.gov/hafe/index.htm. Details, reservations, and equipment rentals for tubing can be obtained from any of several outfitters in the area. One of the oldest and most experienced of these companies is River and Trail Outfitters, www.rivertrail.com/index.php. Be sure to wear a life jacket. You can be fined for tubing without one, and the National Park Service does patrol the river.

Manatees in Chesapeake Bay

Manatees are large marine mammals that look like baking potatoes with whiskers and fins. About once a year, in late summer, one will appear in Chesapeake Bay. Although Florida is the usual northern limit to the range of this animal, each year a few wander northward in search of suitable habitat and a mate. These "sea cows" require warm water, above 72°F, and lots of underwater grasses to eat. In addition, they require fresh drinking water, and so they are often seen at marinas drinking from dripping pipes or hoses. Manatees are gentle creatures. Maryland's most famous manatee visitor, given the name "Chessie," appeared in the Bay for at least two years in the mid-1990s, but has not returned since. There are about 4,000 manatees in Florida, a significant increase from several decades ago. This increase is due to improved awareness of these surprisingly charismatic animals and strict power-boating regulations. The most common cause of death of manatees is injury by the propellers of fast-moving boats.

Showy Flowers of River Banks

The end of July brings into bloom three showy plants that grow along river banks or on the rich alluvial soils left by episodic flooding. One flower is common, one less so, and one very rare indeed.

Joe Pye weed. Joe Pye weed is a common, unmistakable, immense herbaceous plant that can grow as tall as a small tree, as much as twelve feet. A basketball-sized round cluster of pale purple flowers tops the plant, which has leaves arranged in whorls around the stem. The flowers are fragrant, attracting large numbers of butterflies, which flutter in the dappled sun that Joe Pye weed likes best. Joe Pye is the anglicized name that was given to a Native American herbalist who healed early colonists and taught them the uses of local plants. He used extracts of this particular plant to reduce the fevers accompanying typhoid and other diseases. Joe Pye weed has also been used to improve appetite, relax nervous conditions, clear the complexion, and even improve success in courting.

Cardinal flower. This plant has intensely pigmented red flowers and grows in wet soil, particularly along river banks where there is abundant sunlight. The vibrant red flowers grow in upright spikes to a few feet in height. They are pollinated by ruby-throated hummingbirds, about the only pollinator that can reach the base of the long, trumpet-shaped corolla to get the plant's nectar reward, although many others are tempted to try. Old herbals list the dried flower and leaves as being useful for love potions, but in fact the plant contains toxic alkaloids; that euphoric feeling is probably not love but a potentially harmful pharmacological effect.

Turk's cap lily. This member of the lily family is a robust but very rare wildflower bearing brilliant orange flowers and growing best in the rich soil of alluvial floodplains. Count yourself lucky

Cardinal flowers grow in wet soil, especially along streambanks, and attract many kinds of insects and other pollinators.

Turk's cap lilies grow best in the rich, well-drained soils of alluvial floodplains. Robust specimens of the plant may be as much as ten feet tall.

should you encounter one in the wild, especially if it is a healthy specimen standing ten feet in height and bearing up to a hundred flowers. The Latin name says it best: *Lilium superbum*. The six recurved petals are bright orange with purplish spots, and the entire flower is several inches across. While this superb species is found in gardens, it is hard to grow from seeds, so most garden plants were probably dug up and taken from the wild. Perhaps this explains the Turk's cap lily's rarity. Don't confuse this plant with the similar tiger lily, from Asia, which is often found in gardens. The throat of a Turk's cap lily has a green star coloration that distinguishes our native species from the tiger lily.

Where to see Joe Pye weed, cardinal flower, and Turk's cap lily this week: All three plants can be seen along the Big Gunpowder River in Baltimore County and along the Youghiogheny River in Ohiopyle State Park this week.

TRIP OF THE WEEK
Fourth Week of July

Ohiopyle State Park, Pennsylvania

Surrounds of Ohiopyle, Pennsylvania (Fayette County); 46 miles northwest of Frostburg, Maryland

What to see and do: Midsummer is a superb time to visit this recreational and natural wonderland in southwestern Pennsylvania. The Youghiogheny River is the living heart of this 20,500-acre park, a wild river that flows clear and clean through long, slow stretches and over rocks, ledges, and drops that form pounding, dramatic whitewater rapids. From the tiny town of Ohiopyle in the center of the park, visitors can join a professionally guided raft trip through rapids like Cucumber, Dimple, and River's End. Upriver is ten miles of calmer water, ideal for a family float trip. Paralleling the river in the park is twenty-seven miles of the Great Allegheny Passage, a wide, packed limestone trail that runs from Pittsburgh, Pennsylvania, to Cumberland, Maryland. It's perfect for bicycling and has beautiful views of the river and riverbank wildflowers. Naturalists are enchanted by the Ferncliff Penninsula, where hemlocks border the steep slopes along the Yough, shady glens house flowers more typical of Canada than Maryland, and fossil plants can be seen in slabs of sandstone. For those more interested in culture than nature, Fallingwater, architect Frank Lloyd Wright's most famous house, is nearby and open for tours. There's no shortage of things to do at Ohiopyle State Park, and summer temperatures and humidity here are significantly lower than in the Baltimore and Washington metropolitan areas.

Naturalist's tip: The Ferncliff Peninsula Trail, within sight of Ohiopyle Falls, traverses several big blocks of exposed sandstone, some of which have fossilized tree bark plainly visible in them. This area, a National Natural Monument, has good displays of spring and fall wildflowers and is home to species of warblers uncommon in central Maryland.

More information: Visit www.dcnr.state.pa.us/stateparks/finda park/ohiopyle/index.htm.

Cownose Rays and the Chesapeake Ecosystem

It's a hot summer day off Wye Island, and a group of students and I are sorting through subtidal gravels along the Wye River, looking for fossilized shark teeth. One of the students calls our attention to a disturbance offshore, a kind of roiling, swirling of the water, accompanied by small splashing noises. Then we see it, all at the same time: a triangular fin that rises, slices through the water, and then subsides. I can see uncertainty, edged with panic, in a dozen faces, and several students step out of the water onto dry beach. Could it be a shark? Here in mid-Bay, where the water is as much fresh as saline?

But the fin is small, and I quickly realize it is the "wing" of a cownose ray. Everyone who has been to an aquarium has seen rays, beautiful creatures that glide through the water seemingly without effort; but few know that cownose rays are common, even abundant, seasonal residents of Chesapeake Bay. Their numbers have been increasing in recent years, and therein lies a lesson about how species interact and how human interference can upset a delicate balance among the creatures of oceans and bays.

Cownose rays are elasmobranchs, a subclass of fish that also includes skates and sharks. All lack bony skeletons. Instead, flexible support is conferred by cartilage, much as in our nose. All the cartilaginous fish have five to seven lateral gill slits and no air bladders. They must swim continuously in order to maintain the flow of water over their gills, from which they obtain oxygen. Swimming continuously also enables them to maintain buoyancy.

Cownose rays winter off the coast of Florida, but they migrate northward along much of the Atlantic Coast in late spring.

Asiatic Dayflower, the Plant That Made Walt Disney Famous

Blooming now along road edges and other waste places is an unusual-looking flower native to China and Japan but now common here. The Asiatic dayflower has two large oval blue petals above a third, inconspicuous petal and the reproductive structures (stamens and pistils). Popular legend says that when Walt Disney saw this flower he was inspired to create Mickey Mouse, with those iconic large ears and a small face below.

Asiatic dayflowers have a unique appearance, with two oval blue petals above several long curving stamens.

The unusual flower structure of two large petals and one small, is also responsible for the Latin genus name, *Commelina*. Linnaeus named the genus in honor of the Commelijn family—two brothers were successful botanists, while the third was . . . not. In Japan, a blue dye used in specialized kinds of paper production is made from the two large petals. The prominent reproductive structures make this plant a favorite for teaching flower anatomy. Each flower lasts but a day—hence the common name "dayflower."

In the Far East, folk medicine recommends this dayflower to treat sore throats. Extracts of the plant have been shown to have antibacterial and antitussive properties. The plant hyperaccumulates heavy metals, actually extracting them from the soil, making this plant useful in phytoremediation. Asiatic dayflower is quite an interesting plant.

Where to see Asiatic dayflower this week: Road edges and waste places almost anywhere in the state may contain this plant. Asiatic dayflower is common along the C&O Canal towpath, the Northern Central Railroad Trail in Baltimore County, and the Mount Vernon Trail near Alexandria, Virginia, just to name a few. The plant continues flowering until first frost.

Canada Geese Molting

Midsummer is when our resident Canada geese seem to be at their most obnoxious, lingering continually on lawns and in parks and leaving immense amounts of their droppings everywhere. Beaches harboring geese sometimes have to close in August due to high fecal bacteria counts. These problems occur because geese are flightless for about a month, as they grow a new set of feathers to replace the worn and damaged ones of the past year. During this time, Canadas like to loaf and feed on expansive areas of short grass where food is abundant and predators are easily sighted. In addition, they prefer to have water nearby, to which they can escape from terrestrial predators. Canada geese are large animals and are mostly vegetarians, so it takes a lot of forage to support them, especially during molting, which generates high metabolic demands. Because their digestive systems are relatively inefficient at extracting nutrients from that forage, the volume of fecal matter is large. Geese may defecate up to twenty-eight times a day, so watch your step.

Where to see Canada geese this week: Lawns of college campuses such as UMBC, open-space parks, even urban ones such as prey even when they are satiated, and have even been known to accidentally strike at human bathers. Fishermen seeking bluefish on the Bay look for roiled water and vortexes of gulls feeding on shreds of prey fish left by the intense feeding frenzy. Blues fight hard when caught on hook and line. Wire leaders are often used when angling for blues, since they can use their razor-sharp teeth to bite through those made of string.

Bluefish are most common in the lower half of the Bay in late summer. The ones found there tend to be smaller, about a foot long, than those caught in the Atlantic off Maryland beaches. Mature bluefish spawn offshore in midsummer and overwinter off Florida. The species has a worldwide distribution. Blues can live for a dozen years and can weigh up to twenty pounds.

Where to see and catch bluefish this week: Join a charter boat out of any port south of the Bay Bridge, or visit with people fishing the surf at Assateague Island.

Herons Arriving

Maryland marshes host a diverse assemblage of herons, including great blue, little blue, green, and tricolored, as well as great, snowy, and cattle egrets. Only the great blue and green herons, however, are abundant and widespread. The other species are less common and typically nest on remote islands of the Bay. By early to mid-August, great and snowy egrets and tricolor and little blue herons suddenly seem to be much more numerous, especially along the coast. Freshwater ponds on Assateague Island that one day stand quiet and undisturbed are the next day populated by several dozen herons feeding voraciously on the summer's accumulation of small fish. Dawn flights of herons, moving between nighttime roosting sites and daytime feeding areas, become common.

Many of these herons are arriving from locations farther north and west. After a post-breeding dispersal period, they are now reassembling before moving slowly southward with the advancing autumn.

Where to see herons this week: Chincoteague National Wildlife Refuge (Virginia) and Assateague Island National Seashore (Maryland).

American Lotus Flowering

Among the most dramatic flowering plants of shallow freshwater rivers and ponds is the American lotus. Round dark green leaves, as much as two feet in diameter, either float atop the water or are emergent on long stems. The large flower has many white to pale yellow petals, while the pistil has a distinctive "showerhead" structure surrounded by many dozen thread-like stamens. It's an altogether exotic-looking plant that has been naturalized to water gardens due to its great beauty and easy cultivation.

Native Americans once enjoyed the lotus's large rhizome as food. Lotus seeds are also large and are favored by ducks and geese. Those seeds that survive are very long-lived; they may remain dormant for up to a century before germinating when conditions are right. In Maryland, American lotus is confined to just a few locations.

A robust plant of tidal freshwater marshes, the American lotus has large flowers whose pistils resemble old-fashioned showerheads once the petals fall.

Where to see American lotus this week: The most accessible place to see American lotus is Mattingly Park, at Indian Head; from the park's boat ramp, go upstream in your own boat, or rent a canoe or kayak at the park. Another location is at Swan Harbor Farm Park near Havre de Grace.

TRIP OF THE WEEK
Second Week of August

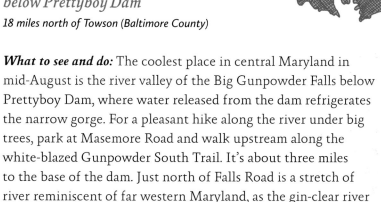

Gunpowder Falls State Park below Prettyboy Dam
18 miles north of Towson (Baltimore County)

What to see and do: The coolest place in central Maryland in mid-August is the river valley of the Big Gunpowder Falls below Prettyboy Dam, where water released from the dam refrigerates the narrow gorge. For a pleasant hike along the river under big trees, park at Masemore Road and walk upstream along the white-blazed Gunpowder South Trail. It's about three miles to the base of the dam. Just north of Falls Road is a stretch of river reminiscent of far western Maryland, as the gin-clear river dances over steep rapids among room-sized boulders and hillsides of mountain laurel. If there is sufficient flow, launch your canoe or kayak from Masemore Road and venture downstream eight miles to Monkton Road through the mature forests of Gunpowder Falls State Park.

Naturalist's tip: The three-mile stretch of river from Masemore Road to the dam is the premier easily accessible fly-fishing venue in the mid-Atlantic region. The parking lot at Falls Road usually holds cars from at least three states. The north-facing hillsides have extensive stands of mountain laurel that bloom for a week or so in late May.

More information: Visit www.dnr.state.md.us/publiclands/central /gunpowder.asp.

Flowering Grasses of Freshwater Marshes

In mid-August, freshwater marshes achieve their peak diversity of plants in flower. That, in turn, brings out many kinds of insects, drawn by pollen and nectar. Plants that are now going to seed attract hungry birds. Our freshwater marshes are busy places on hot summer days. Among the plants drawing attention, three species of flowering grasses are especially notable.

Wild rice. By mid-August, wild rice has mostly already flowered, and now seeds are developing that will soon be ripe for harvest. Of course, beating red-winged blackbirds to the feast is no small task. Huge flocks of these icterids descend on the marshes; they favor wild rice at the "milk" stage, earlier than we humans prefer to harvest. A swirling cloud of noisy blackbirds feeding on the feathery inflorescences of wild rice is a sight worth seeing. Wild rice is an annual plant, so obviously enough seeds escape both birds and humans to repopulate the marsh the next year.

The female flowers of wild rice form at the topmost end of the panicle and ripen earlier than the male flowers, which grow a bit lower on the stem (corn, another familiar grass, ripens in the opposite direction). This difference in timing between female and male ripening generally prevents self-pollination. After fertilization, seeds take about a month to develop, changing from green to the familiar purple-black color of the wild rice we purchase at the food store. Until about 1960, virtually all wild rice was harvested from the wild. It has been domesticated and grown commercially only in the last fifty years.

Common reed. Not every freshwater marsh in Maryland contains wild rice. Conditions must be just right for this grass to flourish. In contrast, the common reed, also known by its Latin congener *Phragmites,* is exceedingly abundant in almost any freshwater marsh anywhere in the state, and even grows in roadside ditches. In fact, any consistently wet low spot in the landscape is subject to colonization by this cosmopolitan invasive. In mid-August, the purple-red feathery seed heads of *Phragmites* tower over the marsh to as high as fifteen feet. By first frost, the inflorescence and stem dry and turn beige; they persist in that state through much of the winter, rustling and rattling in the wind until toppled by heavy snow.

Phragmites spreads vigorously, sending out runners that can grow up to ten feet per season. Roots and rhizomes grow several feet downward and form a dense mat in the soil that prevents other plant species from growing. Within a few years of colonization, a *Phragmites* marsh is often a monoculture, reducing its

Phragmites, *also known as the common reed, is ubiquitous in ditches and wetlands throughout Maryland. The dried inflorescence is often used in autumnal floral arrangements.*

value as wildlife habitat. Unlike wild rice, the seeds of the common reed are rarely eaten by birds. *Phragmites* does have some ecological value: the upright stems provide year-round shelter for animals of the marsh, the roots stabilize erosion-prone soils like those of stormwater treatment ponds, and the seed heads are often used in dried flower arrangements. And stands of common reed make a beautiful sight from spring well into winter.

Cattails. A third well-known grass of freshwater wetlands is cattails. By August, the seed heads, brown, sausage-shaped spikes, are ripe and beginning to shed wind-borne seeds attached to downy parachutes. Cattail down was used by Native Americans as cotton, lining beds, diapers, and moccasins. Dipped in wax, the seed heads can be used as candles or torches. The pollen can be used to thicken soups, and the rhizomes, leaves, and developing flower spike have all been used as food.

Cattails grow quickly and often form dense monocultures in freshwater wetlands. In Florida and California, cattails are considered undesirable invasives that displace native vegetation. Here in the Chesapeake region, cattails rarely take over established marshes, but they will colonize stormwater management ponds, an event generally thought beneficial. Cattails control erosion and remove excess nutrients from water.

Where to see wild rice, common reed, and cattails this week: The extensive marshes along the Patuxent River, especially near Jug Bay, are home to all three species. Close examination will require a boat. You can see common reeds growing side by side with wild rice on the Patuxent River near Jug Bay, but any roadside ditch, stormwater management pond, or freshwater marsh, anywhere in Maryland, likely harbors *Phragmites* and cattails.

May Apple and Jack-in-the-Pulpit: Conspicuous Fruits of Mesic Forests

Among the native wildflowers that fruit now are jack-in-the-pulpit and May apple. Both plants flower in April, and both grow best in the rich soils of undisturbed forest. Their large, conspicuous fruits have been developing slowly over several months and are now mature.

May apple fruits are about an inch long and pale yellow in color. In colonial America, the mature fruits were gathered to make jelly and were highly valued. Nowadays it's rare to see a May apple fruit that has survived hungry animals and insects to reach a soft, squishy maturity in late August. Avoid touching or eating the green portions of May apple plants, because they contain podophyllotoxin, a compound toxic to humans.

Jack-in-the-pulpit fruits are much more likely to survive to maturity, as they contain crystals of calcium oxalate, a chemical that burns the digestive tracts of most animals, including humans. Their bright red color warns hungry animals away. Indeed, some fruits persist until winter, showing an unexpected blotch of color against the snow.

The bright red fruits of jack-in-the-pulpit are easy to locate on the late summer forest floor. The seeds contain crystals of calcium oxalate, which burn delicate throat tissue if ingested.

Where to find May apple and jack-in-the-pulpit this week: Any undisturbed forest statewide, such as those found in Gunpowder Falls, Patapsco Valley,

Tuckahoe, and Cunningham Falls State Parks, harbor these plants. Other good locations include C&O Canal National Historical Park, Sugarloaf Mountain, Patuxent River Park, and the National Arboretum.

Stinging Nettles

Several members of the vegetable kingdom have evolved any number of defenses against being nibbled on, drilled into, mined through, or otherwise assaulted; but few are, well, as nettlesome as the trichomes of *Urtica dioica*, or stinging nettles. Growing along trails and river banks, this robust perennial herb is well able, by late summer, to deliver a burning, itching sting to the exposed skin of any human who ambles by, innocently unaware. For twenty minutes or so, the torture is exquisite until the skin's defenses finally break down the chemicals injected by the syringe-like trichomes (rigid hairs) lining the stems and undersides of leaves of this plant. Among the chemicals injected are the neurotransmitters acetylcholine and serotonin, and the inflammatory response mediator histamine. If stung, treat with hydrocortisone cream or, in a pinch, mud.

Stinging nettles are usually about two feet in height and grow in colonies connected by bright yellow roots and rhizomes. The leaves are triangular in shape with coarsely serrated margins and they grow opposite each other on the stem. Each layer of leaves is offset ninety degrees from the next, giving an ordered appearance. Most diagnostic, however, are the many coarse, spiky trichomes lining the stem. When you see these plants, beware.

Stinging nettles have been used for centuries in folk medicine. Topically, it can be effective in treating arthritis, gout, muscle and joint pain, and eczema. Extracts of the plant contain chemicals that inhibit production of inflammatory cytokines, like tumor necrosis factor and interleukins. In addition, extracts are also used for urinary tract problems and enlarged prostate, and stinging nettles may relieve hay fever symptoms, again through their anti-inflammatory action. Extract of stinging nettle is widely available, but consult a physician before using it.

Stinging nettles also find uses outside of medicine. The young leaves can be boiled and eaten like spinach if picked early in the season, well before flowering. Extracts have been used in shampoos to promote luster, and the intact plant is put in cattle feed to improve coat condition. In England, nettle beer and nettle lemonade have a small rural following. Several species of moth and butterfly caterpillars feed on the leaf tissue.

Knowledge may be power, but all this information will not matter a whit should you stroll bare-legged through a garden of stinging nettles on some woodsy ramble. Take comfort that the pain will soon pass and you'll be more aware of this nettlesome plant on future hikes.

Where to see stinging nettles this week: The rich soils of alluvial floodplains, such as those along the C&O Canal towpath, often host stinging nettles.

TRIP OF THE WEEK
Third Week of August

Potomac River float trip and a visit to Dam Number Four Cave, C&O Canal National Historical Park

12 miles south of Hagerstown (Washington County);
8 miles northwest of Antietam National Battlefield

What to see and do: What better way to relax on a hot late-summer day than floating a few miles down a quiet river, with a stop to explore a cool walk-in cave? Launch your canoe, kayak, raft, tube, or air mattress just below Dam Number Four on the Potomac River in Washington County. Wearing your personal floatation device, you can slip overboard to swim or float along with the slight current to enjoy the clear warm water of late summer. Stop at riffles and ledges to look for clams and snails, or to wet a line, and have lunch under the shade of big riverside silver maples. One mile downriver from Dam Number Four is the mouth of a walk-in cave. It is visible from the C&O Canal towpath if you are walking but requires foreknowledge of where to stop if you are on the river. The accessible portion of Dam Number Four Cave is always at least four feet high, generally only slightly muddy, and runs straight for about a hundred feet, illuminated faintly by sunlight. Bring a flashlight to explore the final several dozen feet, which are in total darkness. Returning to the river, continue drifting down to Taylor's Landing, finishing a slow-paced three-mile float of a relaxing, satisfying river. Hike back to your car on the towpath, or set up a car shuttle before starting the trip.

Naturalist's tip: Look for cave crickets, long-tailed salamanders, and bats in the many nooks and crannies of Dam Number Four Cave (but please do not disturb).

More information: Visit the C&O Canal National Historical Park website at www.nps.gov/choh/index.htm.

· WEEK 4 ·

Japanese Knotweed Flowering

In a walk along any trail or roadside in Maryland you will see an amazing number of plants that are not native to the state. Many are invasive—that is, they outcompete native plants, spread rapidly, flourish, and generally take over the natural landscape. Late August brings into flower a notorious alien invasive, Japanese knotweed.

These shrub-size plants with erect sprays of small white flowers and zigzag, red-flecked stems most often line shady or partly sunny roadsides, forming a dense border. It is a vigorous perennial, sending out roots as much as nine feet down and twenty feet out. These roots have been known to crack concrete and asphalt and undermine the packed clay of flood control berms.

Japanese knotweed is not without beneficial characteristics. It is a commercial source of resveratrol, which is sold as a nutritional supplement. Resveratrol has several interesting but as yet unproven medical effects. It is found in high concentrations

Japanese knotweed is a vigorous, very invasive non-native plant that often grows along the edges of roads and streams.

in the skins of red grapes and the wine made from them (this fact has been proposed to explain the "French paradox": people in France eat a high-fat diet but have low rates of heart disease). In animal experiments, resveratrol has been demonstrated to extend life span, counteract the effects of a high-fat diet, and have anti-cancer, anti-inflammatory, and anti-viral effects. Few of these results have as yet been reported in studies on humans.

Where to see Japanese knotweed this week: Shaded road edges in central Maryland, such as the entrance road to the Avalon area of Patapsco Valley State Park. It is also common along partly shaded river banks, such as those along the Big Gunpowder River.

Ragweed Pollen Counts Peak

Late August brings yet another unpleasantness to sultry days and humid nights: ragweed pollen is being released, causing widespread allergic responses in susceptible individuals. Ragweed allergy, often called "hay fever," is the most common pollen allergy among Maryland residents. Fortunately, modern medicine controls symptoms quite well in most people.

Ragweed is a common plant of late summer, growing in disturbed ground like roadsides, vacant lots, river banks, and fallow fields. The leaves are deeply dissected in a regular pattern. Ragweeds can grow quite tall, up to eight feet in height along stream banks, but are more typically three to four feet high. By August, pollen is being produced in a spike at or near the top of the plant. Each ragweed plant can produce up to a billion pollen grains per year. The pollen is spread by wind and can travel hundreds of miles, staying aloft for days. In the past, individuals with bad ragweed allergies would move to desert areas to escape the torture of hay fever, but as the population has increased and development of land has become more extensive, no part of the United States is free of ragweed pollen.

Some people think their late summer allergies are caused by goldenrods, plants producing bright yellow flowers this time of year, a feature ragweed lacks. However, goldenrod pollen is too heavy to become airborne and is not significantly allergenic.

Where to see ragweed this week: Most people prefer to stay away from this plant, but if you really want to see it, or are on a crusade to eradicate ragweed, you'll find it on any disturbed patch of ground, statewide. Few plants are so common and widespread.

Ghost Crabs Patrol the Beach

Stroll barefoot down the beach at Assateague Island on a late summer night and you may be surprised when something runs across your foot. Is it your imagination? Maybe, but a few steps more and it happens again. Click on your flashlight and you'll soon realize the beach is alive with sand-colored crabs, scuttling everywhere, wonderfully camouflaged so that only their sideways movements betray their presence. They are ghost crabs, aptly named and common on Atlantic beaches.

An adult ghost crab is about two inches across the carapace with a thick squarish body. Like all crabs, it has eight legs; the front two bear pincer-like claws used for capturing and shredding food, while the others are used for walking. Ghost crabs are scavengers, eating carrion, detritus, beach fleas, mole crabs, and small beach clams like *Donax* and *Coquina*. Their eyes are prominent and sit atop eyestalks; their vision is acute. Ghost crabs are mostly nocturnal, but it is not unusual to see one during the early morning or late afternoon. The late-summer beach harbors large numbers of ghost crabs, many of which are small, obviously

By early autumn, hosts of ghost crabs patrol Atlantic beaches at night, gleaning food from both natural sources and trash left behind by beachgoers.

born earlier that year. Winter mortality is high, so many of these small crustaceans won't live to reproduce the next year.

While daytime beachcombers rarely see ghost crabs, they often encounter the crabs' burrows on the forebeach or the dunes. Each hole has a shallow mound of sand and many obvious tracks around it. A burrow can be up to four feet deep, insulating the crab from summer's heat and winter's cold. While ghost crabs are common along most Atlantic coast sandy beaches, they are present in higher numbers on pedestrian beaches than on wilderness beaches. Scientists hypothesize that the trash we humans leave behind provides a supplementary food source for ghost crabs. On beaches where off-road vehicles are allowed, ghost crabs are rare; the traffic collapses their burrows, leading to high mortality.

Where to see ghost crabs this week: Assateague Island beaches.

Assateague Island National Seashore, Maryland and Virginia

9 miles south of Ocean City (Worcester County)

What to see and do: There is something about the late-summer ocean beach: a wistfulness that comes from knowing the season is shifting, that it has in fact almost imperceptibly turned toward autumn. Assateague is a wonderful place to visit at any time of the year, but these last days of August seem especially pleasant, a time to treasure the final bloom of a fading summer. To experience the full character of this barrier island, camp among the dunes at the National Seashore where you can enjoy the magical hours of sunrise and sunset, and walk the ocean beach under the stars.

Naturalist's tip: In summer, biting insects at Assateague can be maddening. They seem worst about five days after a good rain that provides pools of standing water. The best time to visit is after a long dry spell. You can almost always get away from biting insects at the ocean's edge.

More information: Visit www.nps.gov/asis/index.htm.

The Turtles of Midsummer

Hazy, hot, and humid—the three H's of a Maryland summer. The predicted high is 103 in the shade, and the heat index is even higher. Early August in Maryland is not the time to do much of anything outside, but I have signed up for an early evening cruise by canoe on the Tuckahoe, heading upstream from the millpond into the gathering dusk, and I am loathe to cancel. So I load up the canoe, drive ninety minutes to the Eastern Shore, and meet the group on a small beach at a state park. After introductions and instructions, we paddle off, a half-dozen canoes carrying a diverse group of people.

The sun is just above the trees, and its force has been dissipated slightly by the haze and humidity in the air. Still, a sweat pops out instantly on my skin. The quiet waters of the millpond are barely cooler than the air, redolent with the smell of vegetation and mud and decay. Off to the right, a redwing calls, defining its territory; and ahead, the basso thrum of a bullfrog swells the growing chorus of evening birdsong and insect chatter. I am reminded that for the living creatures of this swamp, harsh conditions like heat or rain or sleet are just a normal part of life, to be abided and endured. We humans are the only creatures to complain about the weather.

Still grumpy with the heat, I paddle along. Ahead of us, on a log, a line of red-bellied turtles sit nose to tail; as I approach, each drops into the water with a plop. Only a last brave soul, the largest, waits to bail out until I am only a few feet away. As I glide past the log, I look down into the water to see if any of these turtles is still visible.

And suddenly the magic happens. The millpond water is crystal clear and I can see every detail on the bottom of the creek several feet down. There are turtles down there, in all sizes and shapes, some lying on the bottom, some swimming, some resting on underwater logs. Submerged aquatic vegetation waves in the faint current. Small fish dart in and out of shelter. I am being offered a glimpse into an underwater world that we humans rarely get to see. Usually, these waters are opaque with algae and sediment, impenetrable to our vision, a dense soup that swallows sunlight and hides everything below. Apparently, a long stretch of recent days without rain or wind has permitted the water to clear appreciably. I have never seen such clarity before or since.

This glimpse into life underwater is simply enchanting. It is like looking into an aquarium, but one that is natural and without borders, unmanipulated by humans. Here a crayfish patrols the bottom, there a line of bubbles rising from the mud indicates the damp respirations of some buried mollusk. Diving beetles motor about. And everywhere there are turtles, painted turtles and sliders, spotted turtles and mud turtles, even a few snappers, in a profusion unexpected and startling.

We continue paddling upriver, leaving the millpond and entering riparian forest. Eventually the river begins to widen and unravel into several channels. Promising routes end in tangles of arrowwood and poison ivy, while others just run out of water. Finally, further passage is blocked by a tangle of storm-blown red maples that have fallen across the river. We turn back, floating home over shallows stippled with the shells of freshwater clams, the ribbon-like leaves of wild celery waving in the current. A gray tree frog trills in the gloaming, and far upstream a barred owl hoots its lonesome "who-cooks-for-you" call. The calm of a hot summer's evening settles over the Tuckahoe, and some of that peace settles into the minds and souls of us paddlers. It has been an amazing trip, filled with encounters with wildlife we never could have anticipated. We have ventured into this swamp for recreation and have unexpectedly and happily found re-creation instead.

SEPTEMBER

Pawpaws Ripening

Among our wild fruits, few are as toothsome as a ripe pawpaw, and Labor Day signals the start of a very short harvesting season. The fruit looks like a short, fat banana that changes from green to yellow upon ripening. It tastes like custard, is of about the same consistency, and has several large brown glossy seeds. Ripe pawpaws are hard to find in the wild, since raccoons and other mammals often get to them first. If you are fortunate enough to locate a laden tree, consider yourself lucky, and enjoy. Gently cradle the fruit while it's on the branch. If it falls into your hand, it's ready to eat. Once ripe, pawpaws quickly ferment and become inedible.

Pawpaw plants are small trees or shrubs native to the eastern United States. They prefer moist soil and often grow along

Pawpaw fruits are delicious, tasting like custard, but animals such as raccoons and foxes often harvest the fruits before humans can do so.

slow-flowing streams, where they help stabilize the banks. In recent years, pawpaws seem to have become more common in our forests. One reason for this is because the twigs and leaves are not eaten by whitetail deer. In addition, pawpaws have almost no insect pests, probably because the leaves produce acetogenins, a natural insecticide. One exception is the larvae of zebra swallowtail butterflies. These large and beautiful butterflies require pawpaws exclusively for food in the larval (caterpillar) stage.

Pawpaw flowers appear in early spring, when they are conspicuous against the just-awakening forest. The flowers are bell-shaped, about an inch long, and chocolate-brown in color. They have only a faint scent and are pollinated by carrion flies and fruit flies. Commercial growers of pawpaws sometimes leave rotting meat or fruit nearby in an effort to attract these pollinators.

Where to find pawpaws this week: A reliable location for harvesting ripe pawpaws is along the C&O Canal, where the fruits hanging over the water can be collected by canoe; raccoons seem unwilling to risk a dunking by venturing out to the ends of insubstantial branches.

Nighthawks and Bats at the Ballpark

With a steam-warmed hot dog and a cold beverage in hand and the boys of summer playing under the lights, a visit to the local baseball stadium is a most pleasant way to spend a hot late-summer evening. Most folks don't think of it as a place to experience nature, yet far above the playing field, darting with amazing speed and maneuverability, are two animals that stalk the night skies for insects: nighthawks and bats.

Common nighthawks are slender, long-winged birds displaying tremendously agile flight skills as they capture flying insects with their huge mouths. On the wing, their narrow profile and white underwing patches easily identify them, but even more familiar are their guttural "peent" calls. Nighthawks are rare in Maryland until the migration southward in September, when they stop here on their way to South America.

There are ten species of bats that either breed or pass through Maryland, and identifying them on the wing at the ballpark is virtually impossible. All are extraordinarily agile fliers, with a herky-jerky flight path as they veer to capture insects. Slow-motion photography indicates that bats capture insects in their membranous hindwings, which they use as a net (in contrast to the open-mouthed capture by nighthawks).

While we humans marvel at the aerial acrobatics of both nighthawks and bats, their night-flying insect prey are in one sense even more wonderful than these two vertebrates. Scientists still don't understand fully why insects fly toward lights, be they a lone porch light or the ranks of lamps used to illuminate nighttime baseball games. There are some arcane and difficult-to-understand theories, but it's amazing that this common behavior from such simple animals remains so poorly understood.

Where to see nighthawks and bats this week: Large ballparks lit by floodlights are reliable locations to see both species. The regional major league parks include Camden Yards in Baltimore and Nationals Park in Washington, D.C. Minor league parks in Maryland include Harry Grove Stadium in Frederick, Municipal Stadium in Hagerstown, Regency Furniture Stadium in Waldorf, and Ripken Stadium in Aberdeen. Nighthawks may be present in such places all summer, but they are only common wherever they stop during migration. Bats can be seen at dusk statewide and are surprisingly common, even in suburban and urban areas.

Rock Creek Park

North central Washington, D.C. (See below for specific locations.)

What to see and do: Rock Creek Park, which wanders through our nation's capital, is a surprisingly pleasant place to visit at any season, harboring an unexpectedly wide variety of trees, wildflowers, birds, and mammals. On weekends, Beach Drive is closed to vehicular traffic and makes a fine destination for a bike ride unmolested by Washington's notoriously discourteous drivers. Having been a park for more than a century, it boasts large graceful trees overhanging the roadway, lending cooling shade to cyclists, walkers, and in-line skaters.

Naturalist's tip: There are lovely displays of spring wildflowers in the vicinity of Boundary Bridge, often good birding near the Maintenance Yard, and a fine nature center atop the ridge near Military Road.

More information: The National Park Service, which cares for the park, provides information at www.nps.gov/rocr/index.htm.

· WEEK 2 ·

The Importance of Grasses

Most of our edible grains come from grasses, and the domestication of grasses allowed humans to abandon the life of hunter-gatherers, take up agriculture, and assemble into societies larger than an extended family. The importance of grasses in human culture can hardly be overestimated.

Mid-September is when many species of wild grass come into flower, and Soldiers Delight Natural Environmental Area, in western Baltimore County, may be the best place in the mid-Atlantic states to view a wide diversity of flowering grasses. While blooming wildflowers can be showy, grasses have a subtle beauty that requires a closer look to fully appreciate them. For example, the largest grass at Soldiers Delight, Indian grass, is now in flower, displaying golden-yellow seed

Indian grass is a beautiful native grass that grows up to six feet tall.

heads and leaves turning a bronze color. The most common grass at Soldiers Delight, little bluestem, is also discreetly handsome, with green stems that blend into purple near the base and turn a red-orange in the winter. The individual flowers of grasses are tiny and pollinated by wind rather than insects.

Where to see flowering grasses this week: Soldiers Delight Natural Environmental Area. Stands of grasses can also be seen under power lines throughout Maryland.

Neotropical Songbirds
Passing Through

Early to mid-September marks the peak migration of songbirds that have finished raising young and are now on their way south to the tropics. While the spring migration of these birds northward is a colorful, noisy affair (males in full breeding plumage, singing vigorously), the fall songbird migration is noticeable mostly to birders who spend significant time outdoors in prime habitat. Indeed, few of these birds sing, and in many cases their autumn plumage is drab and camouflaged. Roger Tory Peterson, in his classic *A Field Guide to the Birds,* painted the autumn warblers on two panels he labeled "confusing fall warblers," and that summarizes the situation for beginning and even moderately experienced birders seeking to identify them by species. While some migrating songbirds are present every day between

By the time of the autumn migration southward, many species of birds have lost the bright plumage they wear during breeding season. Contrast the drab fall plumage of this blackpoll warbler with its natty spring garb (see Week 3 of May).

late August and early October, winds out of the north will bring larger numbers that are more easily seen at choke points like Cape May, New Jersey, and Cape Charles, Virginia. Migrants passing through depend on local birds' knowledge to find good food sources, and so they can often be found mixed in with flocks of local birds, like chickadees and tufted titmice.

Migrating songbirds do their flying at night, and on a good night in a quiet location, their chips and call notes can be heard as they pass overhead. Similarly, a telescope or spotting scope aimed at a full moon at this time of year may reveal amazing numbers of birds on their flight south.

Where to see migrating neotropical songbirds this week: Seeing these birds is mostly a matter of weather and wind direction. Under the right conditions, migrating songbirds might be detected almost anywhere in Maryland; but for most species, where they drop down to feed and rest varies. That said, many birds migrate right along the coastline, so Assateague Island is a good place to see and hear migrants, especially at dawn and early evening. Cape May, New Jersey, is another reliable location this week (see "Trip of the Week" below).

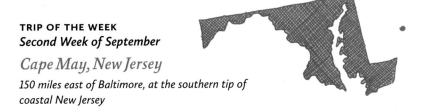

TRIP OF THE WEEK
Second Week of September
Cape May, New Jersey
150 miles east of Baltimore, at the southern tip of coastal New Jersey

What to see and do: A late summer weekend at Cape May is an exhilarating and exhausting place for a visiting birder. There is exciting birding from before dawn to past sunset, in a variety of habitats. The world-renowned Cape May Bird Observatory is a great source of local information and recent sightings. The best place for autumn songbirds is Higbee Beach, where the dawn flight of arriving migrants can be observed from a dike. Other birding hotspots include Cape May Point State Park hawk watch, and the Cape May "Meadows"; just ask for directions from anyone with binoculars.

Naturalist's tip: Winds out of the north bring large numbers of migrants passing through, while winds out of the south will tend to concentrate the birds that can be seen along the coast, because they refuse to risk a crossing of Delaware Bay in the teeth of a south wind. A passing hurricane, even one well off-shore, can bring in unusual vagrant species.

More information: Visit the Cape May Bird Observatory's website at www.birdcapemay.org/.

Broad-winged Hawk Migration

The autumn migration of broad-winged hawks southward is a dramatic affair for those attuned to the sky. It is a predictable event, occurring in a narrow window between September 12 and 25 each year. Only in the past few years have birders realized that the I-95 corridor through Baltimore is a major flyway for this bird. In 2010, broad-winged hawk counts at Cromwell Valley Park, just north of the Baltimore Beltway, exceeded those from world-famous hawk-watching sites like Cape May, New Jersey, and Hawk Mountain, Pennsylvania.

Broad-winged hawks are just a bit smaller than the familiar red-shouldered hawk and significantly smaller than the common red-tailed hawk. A stocky, soaring hawk with a conspicuous banded tail are diagnostic features. Broad-wings nest throughout eastern North America, but the highest densities are in southern Canada and the northern tier of the United States. These raptors nest in dense forests, hunting small rodents from a perch. Only in the fall do broad-wings come to our attention in Maryland, as they become exceedingly common here.

The first cold fronts of September that sweep down from Canada start broad-wings on their migration to Central and South America. In mid- to late morning, as the sun warms the land, air currents called thermals create rising vortexes that soaring hawks such as broad-wings use to gain altitude. They form dramatic "kettles" of circling, soaring, rising hawks that typically comprise a few hundred birds in central Maryland but can contain more than a thousand. At several thousand feet, when the hawks are barely visible to the naked eye, they break out of the thermal and glide southward on the prevailing winds. Losing elevation only slowly, they may soar dozens of miles before locating another updraft of air on which to repeat the process.

With favorable conditions, a broad-wing can cover hundreds of miles in a day without ever flapping its wings, thus conserving energy for the long trip ahead.

Most of us go about our mid-September business without looking up. But from time to time at this season, there can be rivers of birds in the air above us, small dots against the blue sky, making their way south with the wind, on brave journeys that take place in a world beyond our understanding or knowing.

Where to see migrating broad-winged hawks this week: Cromwell Valley Park in Maryland, Hawk Mountain in Pennsylvania, and Cape May in New Jersey are all reliable viewing locations; but under the right conditions, kettles of broad-wings can appear almost anywhere in Maryland.

Monarch Butterfly Migration

The familiar orange and black of monarch butterflies enlivens fields and grasslands all summer, but by late September more and more of these beautiful insects fill our skies. While several butterfly species migrate, none do so in such famously large numbers, and so conspicuously, as monarchs. On rare occasions, with adverse wind and weather conditions, immense numbers of monarchs can pile up at choke points on their migration route, awaiting favorable circumstances for crossing a large body of water. For example, on September 20, 2010, an estimated half-million monarchs filled every bush, tree, and telephone wire in Cape May, New Jersey.

Butterflies are certainly the most beautiful and charismatic order of all the insects, and monarchs may be the most beloved species of *Lepidoptera*. Even to the most unemotional scientist, monarch butterflies are wondrous, evoking a sense of awe at their complex life history and incredible migration. After decades of research, much still remains completely mysterious about the continentwide annual journey of this seemingly simple organism.

Monarchs in Maryland go through two or three generations over the course of the summer. The month-long larval (caterpillar) stage feeds exclusively on milkweed, while adults sip flower nectar over their two- to six-week lifespans. In September, probably in response to shortening day length, the year's final brood of adults fails to mature sexually, feeds voraciously to store fat, and begins to migrate southward. Over the next two months, each monarch will join a swelling throng that may eventually number one hundred million, a virtual river in the air of orange confetti in search of exactly the right conditions for surviving winter. The destination is a few square miles on twelve mountaintops in the Mexican state of Michoacan, where the monarchs will take up residence, packed tightly among the branches of oyamel firs. The temperature and humidity in Michoacan are just right for these creatures to preserve life in a state of torpor, awaiting the lengthening days and warming temperatures of spring. No one understands how such simple animals can find these same remote glades among such a huge landscape year after year, without any guide or memory or experience (the individuals who make the trip are a couple of generations removed from those who made it the previous year). No scientist understands how monarchs have evolved to migrate such large distances when fellow insects migrate only short distances or do not migrate at all. Furthermore, no one understands how shortening days translate into an inhibition of sexual maturity, or how they evoke the urge to migrate. We poorly understand how their metabolism can suddenly shift from supporting the rigors of migration to the state of torpor which they quickly adopt upon arrival and how life can be sustained for months in this quiescent state. Barely do we understand how migrants, whether butterflies or birds, sense direction and do route-finding. Indeed, for all the familiarity of monarch butterflies, their migration is a mystery wrapped in an enigma encased in a conundrum, and truly one of the wonders of our natural world.

Where to see monarch butterflies in migration this week: Monarch caterpillars are found in any open field across the state that has milkweed plants. Adult butterflies are more catholic in diet, feeding on a wide diversity of flowers and so may be found anywhere statewide. By mid-September, many adults head south. Large numbers have been noted migrating along ridgelines such as at Washington Monument State Park, in Frederick County. Regionally, the best places to view significant concentrations of migrating monarchs are choke points like Cape May, New Jersey; Point Lookout, Maryland; and Cape Charles, Virginia, when wind direction is from the south.

Tickseed Sunflower Blooming

Late summer and early fall bring a spectacular display of tickseed sunflowers to our freshwater marshes. Lining the edge of the marsh where low tide exposes the mud flats and high tide inundates roots, tickseed sunflower blooms in a profusion equaled by few wildflowers, terrestrial or aquatic. While individual flowers have only a faint scent, the immense numbers and den-

Tickseed sunflowers brighten ditches and freshwater wetlands in early fall. Their seeds have hooked barbs that attach to clothing or fur, an effective dispersal mechanism.

sity of plants yield a delicate fragrance and attract a variety of autumn pollinators, especially bees and butterflies. The nectar or pollen of the tickseed sunflower is thought to be a reliable and important food source for migrating monarch butterflies.

If you don't have a canoe or kayak to get out onto our freshwater marshes to see tickseed sunflower, don't despair; this hardy and common plant also enlivens roadside ditches throughout the coastal plain. Tickseed sunflower seeds cling to fur, feathers, and pant-legs with equal tenacity, and therefore spread far and wide, growing anywhere that has sufficiently moist soil.

Where to see tickseed sunflowers this week: Freshwater marshes such as those along the Patuxent River, especially at Jug Bay, host many tickseed sunflowers, but on the Eastern Shore even roadside ditches typically grow enough plants to brighten the autumn landscape.

TRIP OF THE WEEK
Third Week of September

Jug Bay area, Patuxent River
8 miles southeast of Upper Marlboro (Prince George's County)

What to see and do: Jug Bay is the scenic and biotic heart of the Patuxent River, and mid- to late September may be the best time to visit and experience this beautiful freshwater marsh. Your options for exploration are many and varied. If you have your own canoe, kayak, or small boat, launch at Selby's Landing near Croom. To explore the intricate web of tiny channels that drain into a freshwater marsh, paddle directly across the river into House Creek, and go upriver until you run out of water. There, with the tall vegetation enveloping your boat on both sides (spiders dropping into your canoe), you can experience what it's like to be a part of a marsh. For a longer trip, turn right (south, downstream) as you leave Selby's Landing. The first major tributary on the right is Mataponi Creek, whose extensive marshes harbor wetland plants such as wild rice, pickerelweed, Walter's millet, and water hemlock, and a variety of marsh birds. Jug Bay Wetlands Sanctuary, on the east side of Jug Bay, sponsors canoe explorations for those without a boat of their own.

If you prefer dryshod hiking, Patuxent River Park, on the west side of Jug Bay, has miles of trails, many of them overlooking the marsh, and several boardwalks through the wetlands. Cyclists and hikers may want to pedal or walk the nearby Critical Areas Driving Tour, which is also open to motor vehicles, but on Sundays only.

Naturalist's tip: The tidal surge in Jug Bay can be quite significant, so if you are in a canoe, avoid paddling against the tide. The extensive marshes host a good nesting population of least bitterns, a long-necked wading bird uncommon elsewhere in Maryland. It is just one of many bird species that frequent these marshes, especially during spring and fall migration.

More information: For more on Selby's Landing, visit www .patuxentwatertrail.org/site40.html. Jug Bay Wetlands Sanctuary is the best source for information about the Patuxent's living things; see www.jugbay.org. Information on the extensive lands of Patuxent River Park may be found at http://www.pgparks.com /page332.aspx. Details about the Critical Areas Driving Tour may be found at www.dnr.state.md.us/publiclands/drivepg.asp.

· Week 4 ·

Chimney Swifts

It's a pleasant late September evening, the sun has just gone down, and the sky is tinged with pink clouds contrasting against the ever-deepening blue. A chorus of twitterings overhead fills in the gaps between the noise of traffic and the general din of urban life as a swirl of birds circles the old school. Their shape shifts like smoke on a breezy day, individual birds breaking loose from the flock from time to time. It's an amazing sight, and no one nearby is paying the least attention. These are chimney swifts, long-winged, big-mouthed birds often described as "cigars with wings." But that descriptor hardly does justice to their sweet song, energetic flight, and gentle demeanor.

As dusk descends, the flock flies lower and in a more coherent fashion. One bird breaks off and flies downward into the brick chimney of the old school. Within a few seconds, a second, a third, and a fourth follow. Suddenly, the entire flock of several hundred birds disappears, in a stream, into the chimney, and within a minute the sky is empty of birds.

While chimney swifts are common throughout Maryland in summer, each pair nesting in their own chimney, the autumn migration brings much larger numbers to communal roosts in large chimneys. Here the birds cling to the vertical sides of the chimney with strong anisodactyl clawed feet, huddling close in inclement weather and departing at first light. In precolonial times, the numbers of chimney swifts were smaller, because of a dearth of natural nesting sites in hollow trees. Although now common in the eastern United States, in the past twenty years there has been a population decline as more and more chimneys are torn down or sealed off. Chimney swifts are true long-distance migrants, overwintering in the Amazon basin.

Where to see chimney swifts this week: In the Baltimore area, abandoned factory chimneys, like those along the Jones Falls in Hampden, have been reliable places to see large flocks of chimney swifts during migration. In Washington, D.C., chimneys of apartment buildings in Cleveland Park have hosted swifts. The chimneys the birds use, however, often seem to change from year to year, so the best advice is to survey a number of old large chimneys at dusk and hope you get lucky enough to see this startling behavioral phenomenon.

Chestnut Oak Acorns Falling

Among the many species of oak found in Maryland, chestnut oaks are notable for their large, handsome acorns. Oval in shape, often more than an inch long, and having a yellow or yellow-green upper hemisphere, these robust acorns are a valuable food for wildlife, including turkeys, squirrels, deer, and chipmunks. Not every year yields a good acorn crop, however. Chestnut oaks put out a large number of acorns (up to 300 pounds per mature tree) only every four to five years, whereas white oaks mast significantly every two to three years. Chestnut oak acorns germinate in the fall, so they do not require a period of dormancy or cold.

Chestnut oaks are the dominant tree on dry ridge-tops in Maryland, tolerating

Chestnut oaks are common on ridge-tops in Maryland, and produce large, colorful acorns.

xeric soils that are often nutrient poor as well. They are often damaged by gypsy moths, insects whose larval stage prefers oak leaves as a food source. Chestnut oaks are easily identified by the leaf, which is shallowly lobed like white oak but with more lobes (10–15), reminiscent of the now-extirpated chestnut tree. In addition, the bark of chestnut oaks is massively and deeply ridged. The bark of chestnut oak has a high tannin content and is still used to cure leather.

Where to see chestnut oaks this week: The Appalachian Trail runs along the ridge of South Mountain, and chestnut oaks are common there. The High Knob picnic area of Gambrill State Park in Frederick County also has many of these trees shading tables and pavilions. Chestnut oaks are common. Many old suburban neighborhoods and parks west of Chesapeake Bay harbor this lovely oak.

TRIP OF THE WEEK
Fourth Week of September

South Fork of the Shenandoah River for canoeing and canoe camping

10 miles southwest of Front Royal, Virginia (Warren County)

What to see and do: Late September is typically the most reliably pleasant weather of the year in the mid-Atlantic region: days are delightfully warm and sunny, nights are agreeably cool, and rivers run low but clear. Summer is fading. Riverside sycamores are already losing their leaves, while the last wildflowers are still blooming. It's the perfect time to canoe a mountain river like the Shenandoah, camping overnight along the way. The nicest section along the Shenandoah is the twenty-eight miles between Bixler Bridge (downstream of Luray) and Bentonville, where the scenery is mostly pastoral and forested, with the mountains of the Massanutten Range often in view. Camping is available on national forest land on the left side of the river or at several private campgrounds on river right.

Naturalist's tip: Much of the Shenandoah Valley is underlain by limestone, creating numerous caves in a karst topography, characterized by steep ravines, sinkholes, and caves. Soils are "sweet" rather than acidic, a condition favored by many native wildflowers. Look for columbine and hepatica in sheltered areas of thick soil, as well as New York aster growing from cracks in the massive cliff at Compton.

More information: Downriver Canoe Company (www.downriver .com/) is just one of several outfitters nearby who can supply canoes, shuttles, and information. Downriver also leases camping sites, in the meadow at the foot of Compton Cliff.

summer outside western Maryland is likely to be the similar but slightly larger Cooper's hawk. Around here, sharpies are more common in winter, especially in the eastern half of Maryland, where they often hunt small birds at feeders.

Where to see sharp-shinned hawks this week: While Hawk Mountain, Pennsylvania, and Cape May, New Jersey, are superb locations for seeing sharpies this week, Cromwell Valley Park just north of Baltimore is also a fairly good spot. This time of year, there often are experienced birders at the Cromwell hawkwatch platform who can help you find hawks and assist you with identification.

TRIP OF THE WEEK
First Week of October

Hawk Mountain

61 miles northeast of Harrisburg, Pennsylvania;
10 miles north of Hamburg, Pennsylvania (Berks County)

What to see and do: The annual fall migration of raptors is one of the most dramatic natural phenomena in the mid-Atlantic, and Hawk Mountain Sanctuary is perhaps the best place to view large numbers of these birds of prey on their autumnal trip south. Located in east-central Pennsylvania, the 2,600-acre private, nonprofit facility features panoramic views over the Schuylkill Valley and along the spine-like Kittatinny Ridge. In the fall, raptors, such as hawks, eagles, falcons, and vultures, tend to get funneled along this ridge, using updrafts and prevailing winds to speed their migration southward. On a good day, more than a dozen species and several thousand individuals may pass the two lookouts, some birds coming so close that binoculars are not needed. Visitors cannot help but be impressed by the sheer speed and strength of these beautiful birds. The first week in October is when sharp-shinned hawk numbers peak, but any time between mid-September and December can, with the right winds, yield an enjoyable day afield watching raptors. The Visitor Center has interesting and informative displays and programs to aid your understanding and enjoyment of these birds.

Naturalist's tip: Be sure to dress warmly. The lookouts are on exposed ridges that are always colder than might be anticipated. Bring a seating pad for the hard rocks of the lookouts, and bring binoculars. An official "counter" is always present, an employee who is an expert in raptor identification. If you sit nearby, some counters may share what they are seeing by calling out names of birds as they spot them (but do not interrupt the counter's work).

More information: Contact www.hawkmountain.org.

Stink Bugs Preparing for Winter

The fall colors are looking better daily and a cold front moved through last night, so a visit to the hawk watch at Washington Monument State Park in Frederick County is in order. From the ridgetop monument there are fine views of the countryside in all directions, but with the wind out of the west today there are few hawks. Instead there are lots of bugs, marmorated stink bugs. At first the bugs are not noticeable, as their marbled appearance blends with the native stone of the monument. Soon, however, one crawls across your bare skin. Then you notice a dozen of them on your pant leg, and you quickly realize that the monument is literally awash in these bugs. They cluster in cracks and pile up in the lee of the wind, while underfoot their deceased brethren crunch like popcorn. On a warmer, less windy day, the smell would be unpleasant—stink bugs are aptly named.

Marmorated stink bugs are natives of Asia who were first identified near Allentown, Pennsylvania in the late 1990s. Having left behind in Asia their usual predators and parasites, marmorated stink bugs reproduced rapidly, and quickly became pests. They feed on more than seventy species of plants, and fruit trees are especially affected; stink bugs are most numerous in the fruit-growing regions of the Cumberland and Shenandoah Valleys. Like all true bugs, marmorated stink bugs are vegans, eating only plants. They use piercing mouthparts to inject enzymes into fruits and then to suck out the resulting liquid.

Marmorated stink bugs are easily identified by their shield-shaped thorax, which is marbled gray in color, and the white bands on their antennae and legs. As the weather cools, these bugs seek shelter where they might overwinter. They get into houses by ill-fitting windows, vents, and soffits, and seem especially adept at such home invasions. The simplest way to deal with them is to allow them to crawl onto a piece of paper and then take them outside for release.

Where to see marmorated stink bugs this week: You've probably already seen these pests. As the weather cools, if you haven't had any stink bugs in your house, you probably soon will. If you wish to study larger collections of them, go to the ridges on either side of the Cumberland Valley, like Washington Monument State Park, which harbor large concentrations of stink bugs.

Canada Geese Arriving

We hear them before we see them: an unmistakable chorus of gabbling notes, mixing with each other in a random cacophony that is somehow symphonic. We look up to see a staggered V-shaped line of geese, long necks outstretched as if straining toward their goal, winging southward, ever southward. The migration of Canada geese into the Chesapeake is perhaps the most beloved of the early signs of fall, a tradition eagerly anticipated by generations of Marylanders, who pause from their daily activities to stand dumbfounded, gazing upward in wonder and awe at this symbol of freedom arriving unheralded from wild, untrammeled places.

In recent decades that sense of wonder has been eroded, because Canada geese are now familiar animals of pond, park, and lawn, present throughout the calendar year. Of the several hundred thousand Canadas that winter in Maryland, about half are year-round residents. These birds tolerate humans, coexist with us side by side, and can even be pests when they leave their copious droppings on sidewalks and lawns. Wild Canada geese behave differently. They are wary to an extreme degree, as any waterfowl hunter can tell you, exhibiting a keen intelligence and avoiding any situation that impresses them as out of the ordinary or in any way associated with humans.

Canada geese are monogamous, making a life-long pair bond. Migration is usually in family flocks of related individuals. Birds arriving in the Chesapeake Bay region in October have typically spent the summer in Labrador, Canada, on the Ungava Peninsula, where they nest on the treeless tundra. Under favorable weather conditions, geese may make that entire 700-mile journey in about a day, without stopping, but they can take up to a week to complete the trip. The spring migration in March is more saltatory, as the birds travel intermittently, following the northward-retreating snow line.

Where to see Canada geese this week: Just look up, especially on mornings when there are blue skies and winds out of the north. The arriving geese congregate at refuges like Merkle Wildlife Sanctuary, in Prince George's County, and Blackwater National Wildlife Refuge, in Dorchester County.

Pokeweed Fruits Turn Purple

Few wild fruits are as distinctive as the purple-black berries of pokeweed. Used by generations of kids as "warpaint" and by Civil War soldiers as a source of ink for writing letters home, pokeweed fruits are unmistakable. That's useful, because all parts of this robust perennial are toxic, containing the alkaloid phytolaccine.

Pokeweed is a widespread and common weed of waste places, fencerows, and fallow gardens. Small leaves emerge in early spring from the young shoot. As long as no red coloration is showing, the leaves can be boiled three times to yield the classic southern potherb "poke salad." Although a popular dish in much of Dixie, even the youngest leaves have low levels of toxins,

Pokeweed fruits are poisonous to humans if eaten, but harmless to many kinds of birds, who enjoy the pulpy, purple fruit.

and so nutritionists advise against eating this leafy vegetable at any time of year. By midsummer, poke is often three to six feet high. A raceme of small greenish-white flowers appears later, eventually developing into the purple fruits. By mid-November, birds have happily eaten the berries; they are unaffected by the toxin.

Where to see pokeweed this week: Pokeweed grows in weedy locations such as fencerows and is very common. Urban parks like Leakin Park in Baltimore and Rock Creek Park in Washington, D.C., contain it, as do vacant lots and less-than-manicured backyards.

TRIP OF THE WEEK
Second Week of October

Great Allegheny Passage by train and bicycle
Cumberland and Frostburg

What to see and do: Fall color in Maryland just doesn't come any better than the mountains of Allegany and Garrett Counties. A unique and pleasant way to enjoy this annual spectacle is to combine bicycling with a scenic train ride. The Western Maryland Scenic Railroad travels sixteen miles uphill from Cumberland to Frostburg, cutting through the Allegheny Front at the Narrows, around the photogenic Helmstetter's Curve, and through the 914-foot-long Brush Tunnel. The trip uses either a restored diesel engine or a beautiful 1916 Baldwin 2-8-0 steam locomotive. A small extra fee is charged for your bicycle. Once at the turnaround point in Frostburg, mount your bicycle and return to Cumberland on the Great Allegheny Passage, a crushed limestone path that occupies the right-of-way of the old Western Maryland Railroad. The best part of this bike ride is that it's all downhill, dropping about 600 feet on a grade that never exceeds 1.5 percent.

Naturalist's tip: Railroad rights-of-way provide habitat for wildflowers that prefer sunny conditions and dry soil. Look for plants like butter-n-eggs, goldenrod, and asters. These plants also attract butterflies and less colorful but interesting insects.

More information: For more on the Western Maryland Scenic Railroad, visit www.wmsr.com. For more information on the Great Allegheny Passage, visit www.atatrail.org.

Wild Fruits Ripening

The onset of cold nights, and perhaps the first frost of the season, brings the fruits of several wild plants into maturity. The result is a cornucopia of berries and fruits enjoyed by wildlife as they fatten up for winter.

Wild cranberries. Wild cranberries are not common throughout Maryland, but frost pocket bogs in Garrett County harbor these tart, delectable berries. When the fall color tourist season winds down, local residents sneak out to their favorite cranberry bog with bucket in hand to harvest berries that will grace the Thanksgiving table in another month.

Asiatic tearthumb. This plant, also known as mile-a-minute vine, is an aggressive invasive annual vine common in much of Maryland. Its only redeeming value is that the unique sky-blue berry is eaten by a variety of birds. Unfortunately, the birds then spread the seeds. The two common names of this plant are accurate descriptors. Sharp, downward-pointing barbs along the stem make manual removal of the plant painful and difficult. Mile-a-minute vine grows as much as six inches a day, allowing it to spread aggressively and form dense mats atop other plants. This plant needs direct sunlight and moist soil, so it grows well in riparian areas. Asiatic tearthumb escaped from a nursery in York, Pennsylvania, in the 1930s and has since spread throughout the northeastern states.

Persimmons. Persimmons are fairly common small trees that grow in sunny locations as diverse as islands in the midst of freshwater marshes and the dry soils of serpentine barrens. Their fruits, apricot in color and about the size of a golf ball, are typically edible only after frost. Captain John Smith, who explored the Chesapeake Bay in the early 1600s, wrote of persimmons, "If it not be ripe it will drawe a mans mouth awrie with much

Asiatic tearthumb is an aptly named invasive vine that can form impenetrable curtains over shrubs, small trees, and herbaceous vegetation.

torment." Captain Smith had it right; before frost, the fruit is astringent and "furry" tasting, due to the presence of soluble tannins. Frost breaks down cell walls, leading to a chemical change in the tannins that converts them to an insoluble form and removes the astringency. If you can beat the racoons, squirrels, and birds to a ripe persimmon, you'll enjoy its wild flavor, which differs from that of the cultivated persimmons found in supermarkets.

Where to find cranberries, asiatic tearthumb, and persimmons this week: Wild cranberries are common in Cranesville Bog in extreme western Maryland (part of the bog is actually in West Virginia). Asiatic tearthumb is very abundant along roads and trails in many of our parks, such as Patapsco Valley State Park and Rock Creek Park. Persimmon trees grow as widely scattered individuals and do not produce fruits every year, so you have to keep your eyes open to find this tree. The C&O Canal towpath is one possibly productive location.

Prime Fall Color in Western Maryland

Fall color comes to the higher elevations of western Maryland late in the second week or early in the third week of October. There are often days during this week in Garrett County that are frosty and crisp when the rest of Maryland is still enjoying summery weather. The chilly temperatures speed the formation of red pigments in leaves. Sugar maples are arguably the most colorful tree in the autumn forest, displaying red, orange, and yellow leaves; sugar maples constitute a significant proportion of the forest on the Appalachian Plateau.

Where to see prime fall color in western Maryland this week:
Almost any forest in western Maryland is ablaze in color this week, but those in Swallow Falls and Big Run State Parks, and the Garrett, Potomac, and Green Ridge State Forests cover large tracts of unbroken forest and contain the full palette of autumn hues. Closer to the metropolitan areas of central Maryland, the parks of the Blue Ridge (Cunningham Falls and Gambrill State Parks, Catoctin Mountain Park, and the Frederick City watershed) reach peak color in the third week of October, a bit earlier than forests at lower elevations.

Cottony Seeds Blowing in the Wind

Plants broadcast their seeds using a variety of mechanisms. Cranberries, tearthumbs, and persimmons attract animals by their colorful and nutritious fruits. The seeds encased within the fruits are excreted from the animals in a new location, and with a dollop of natural fertilizer to boot. Other plants use the wind to spread their seeds, carried aloft on silk-like hairs that catch the breeze.

Milkweed seedpods. These seed pods are now splitting open, releasing a large but lightweight seed attached to a number of long filamentous hairs. On a windy day, these seeds can travel great distances. Milkweed seeds prefer disturbed soil and full sun, growing into robust perennial plants. The mature plant is distinctive, being a pale green in color and exuding a milky latex from its stems. Milkweeds are the exclusive food plant for monarch butterfly larvae. Milkweed seeds floating on the wind can be a beautiful sight.

Groundsel tree. Groundsel is a shrub common at the upland edge of salt and brackish marshes; it produces many seeds attached to white bristles. The seeds are released in mid- to late autumn, blowing around the marsh like an early snowstorm.

Where to find milkweeds and groundsel trees this week: Milkweeds are very common in fallow fields throughout Maryland. Groundsel tree is not as well known, but it populates virtually every brackish marsh on Maryland's Eastern Shore, including Blackwater National Wildlife Refuge, Assateague Island National Seashore, and even the eastern approaches to the Chesapeake Bay Bridge.

TRIP OF THE WEEK
Third Week of October

Old Rag Hike, Shenandoah National Park

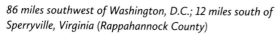

86 miles southwest of Washington, D.C.; 12 miles south of Sperryville, Virginia (Rappahannock County)

What to see and do: On any short list of great hikes in our national parks, Old Rag is often near the top. Separate from the main ridge of Shenandoah National Park, Old Rag Mountain is traversed by a strenuous eight-mile hiking trail that features panoramic views, difficult rock scrambling, significant elevation change, and more fun than almost any other trail in the mid-Atlantic. The main attraction of the hike occurs between mile two and three, where the trail passes through narrow clefts between rocks, along ledges with airy drop-offs, over piles of boulders the size of cars or houses, and even underneath rock at least once. Dramatic views abound, some of which feature 360-degree views of the surrounding Virginia countryside. Many hikers who make an annual pilgrimage to Old Rag do so in mid- to late October to view the fall color. Whatever the season, what- ever the reason, Old Rag is always rewarding. One caveat: this is a very popular hike, so arrive at the trailhead before 8:00 A.M., because parking is limited and the footpath gets crowded.

Naturalist's tip: While the fall color on Old Rag is justifiably famous, early May brings into bloom a wonderful diversity of colorful native wildflowers. Trillium, wild geranium, wild ginger, and even some native orchids are just a few of the species present.

More information: Visit www.nps.gov/shen/planyourvisit/old-rag -hike-prep.htm.

Brook Trout Spawning

Shortening days and cooler water temperatures stimulate breeding in Maryland's only native trout species, brook trout. Requiring pristine water quality, forested stream banks, and an all but undeveloped watershed, brook trout are a barometer of the ecological integrity and health of those few remaining small streams in Maryland that still harbor the species.

Most of us think of fish as dull in color, camouflaged in hues of earth and water, but brook trout are handsome fish whose lower flanks glow red and orange in the breeding season. Choosing a section of stream that has riffles to provide oxygenated waters and a gravel substrate to supply cover, a female scoops out a shallow nest, called a redd, that may be a foot in diameter. She lays eggs and they are fertilized by an attending male; she then covers them with gravel, creating a place where young embryos can develop slowly but in safety over the winter.

In Maryland, brook trout are mostly confined to about 380 miles of very narrow headwater streams. Many of these creeks you could spit or jump across, and you might never suspect that they host fish almost a foot long. However, many of these headwater brook trout populations are isolated from each other, separated by stream reaches that have unfavorable physical characteristics (like too high water temperature) or biotic factors (like predatory brown trout and smallmouth bass). Such small and isolated populations are more likely to go extinct, and recolonization would be unlikely.

Why are brook trout confined to tiny headwater streams? In precolonial times, brookies occupied large sections of creeks and rivers. Watersheds were almost entirely forested, which reduced sediment runoff and kept water temperatures cool. As humans occupied and developed more of the landscape, water quality declined. We know that if more than 0.5 percent of the land area in a watershed has impervious surfaces (like buildings, parking lots, and roads), brook trout numbers will be greatly reduced; extinction is certain at just 4 percent. In response to development, brook trout have moved upstream to the only remaining sections of favorable habitat, where they are now permanently isolated. Only in western Maryland are there a few watersheds pristine enough to harbor a network of interconnected streams, where brook trout live much as they did in precolonial times.

Where to see brook trout this week: The headwater streams of the Little Savage River in western Maryland form the Free State's largest complex of pristine habitat for brookies.

Prime Fall Color in Central Maryland

During October, the fall colors descend from the mountains, and by the fourth week of the month a visual symphony of colors has reached the trees of central Maryland. The forests here are dominated by oaks, whose leaves turn from green directly to russet brown and turn a bit later than most other Maryland trees, delaying prime fall color here compared to the maples of the Blue Ridge and Appalachian Plateau and the sycamores and birches of the river valleys. Although weather can delay or speed up the appearance of fall color, and can affect the intensity of the colors, the reliability with which fall color peaks sometime in this week implies that the process is triggered by the longer nights of autumn rather than by weather.

During the growing season, most leaves are green, because they contain high concentrations of chlorophyll, the pigment primarily responsible for photosynthesis. Most plants also have yellow, carotenoid, pigments in their leaves, which help absorb wavelengths of light that chlorophyll does not. Carotenoids also protect the chemical reactions in plant cells from being damaged by oxygen radicals created during conditions of excess light; however, the yellow to orange color of carotenoid pigments are masked by the green of chlorophyll. In autumn, deciduous plants begin to break down and resorb the chlorophyll in their leaves, so that this valuable biological chemical will not be lost to the environment upon leaf fall. Carotenoids are much slower to break down, so their color becomes visible to our eyes when the chlorophyll disappears.

Red colors come from still another class of pigment, anthocyanins. Anthocyanins are not present in tree leaves during the growing season but are synthesized about the same time that chlorophyll is resorbed. Sugar concentrations in leaves increase in the fall and are used as the building blocks for anthocyanin synthesis. Whether a leaf is red, orange, or yellow depends on the relative concentrations of carotenoids and anthocyanins. The browns present in oak leaves come from tannins. Unlike chlorophyll, these other pigments stay with the dying leaf and are thus lost to the tree as a source of fixed carbon for growth in the following year.

In general, leaf colors are most intense when October has dry sunny days and cool dry nights. Both conditions promote the synthesis of anthocyanins. Of course, the tree has to be in good condition in the first place, having received sufficient but not too much water during the growing season and not having suffered significant insect or fungal damage. That's a scientific explanation of fall color, but such words can never capture the sheer beauty of a line of trees glowing red, orange, and yellow in late October sun.

Where to see fall color in central Maryland this week: There is often excellent fall color nearby, even in heavily developed central Maryland, during the few days of the prime season, so by the fourth week of October there's no need to go far afield. Some favorite spots in central Maryland are the National Arboretum and the Gunpowder River valley.

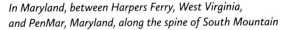

Appalachian Trail hike

In Maryland, between Harpers Ferry, West Virginia, and PenMar, Maryland, along the spine of South Mountain

What to see and do: The Appalachian Trail (AT) is the most famous footpath in the world, and we have about forty miles of its 2,181-mile length in Maryland. Fall is a wonderful time of year to experience the AT. The cool days of autumn make hiking a delight, and views from atop the Blue Ridge open up as the leaves fall. While Maryland's portion of the AT is considered the easiest of any state's, there are still plenty of ups and downs, especially where roads cross the trail at "gaps." Among the most scenic portions of Maryland's AT are the Potomac River gorge near Harpers Ferry; the civil war battlefields at Turner, Fox, and Crampton Gaps; and the dramatic overlooks at Annapolis Rocks and High Rock. The lore of the AT is fascinating. Every year, several hundred hikers complete the entire length of the trail in a "through hike," and a few meet the "Four-State Challenge," which includes transiting Maryland in one day. Just over the border in Pennsylvania, many through hikers meet the "Half-Gallon Challenge" at Pine Grove Furnace, consuming a full half-gallon of ice cream in one sitting, a feat of gluttony inconceivable to anyone who doesn't hike every day for months.

Naturalist's tip: The Appalachian Trail in spring offers a variety of wildflowers, including trailing arbutus and pink lady's slipper orchids. Beautiful displays of mountain laurel bloom in late May along the entire length of the trail in Maryland.

More information: Visit the Appalachian Trail Conference at www.appalachiantrail.org. Its headquarters and visitor center are in nearby Harpers Ferry, West Virginia, and are worth a visit. For information on Maryland's portion of the AT, visit www.dnr .state.md.us/publiclands/at.asp.

Autumn River

The river takes us. We had been floating along without care, but now the current has picked up and the riverbed rocks slide by soundlessly under the hull with increasing speed. I straighten the canoe so that the bow points downriver, directly into the vee, and waves slap the sides as we bounce down the riffle and into the calm water below. Far down in this deep pool, giant carp, robust and fully two-feet long, are dark shadows, cruising along with nose into the current, their piscine existence limited by the shoals and rocky shelves that define this pool.

Fall is coming on, and for more than twenty autumns we have bid farewell to warm weather with a late October cruise on the Shenandoah River. The riverside maples and birches glow yellow in the afternoon sun, infused with a brilliance that we know will be transitory. The air is warm, and if we didn't know better, we might think that Indian summer was a permanent condition. But in another week, the trees will be bare of leaves and the first chill rain of autumn will blow sideways on a northerly wind. Because we know the inevitability of the change of seasons, this day of endings has a wistfulness to it, a sense that all living things are winding down.

What little current there is pushes us around a bend, and ahead is Golden Rock, a cliff of limestone that glows in the late afternoon sun. The sound of rushing water comes to us, and we see splashes of white dancing above the river's horizon line. Being familiar with the river, we know that the cliff amplifies the river's noise and that the rapid is just a straightforward and bouncy wave train, unencumbered by rocks and holes and pourovers. We paddle through; only one wave dumps over the gunwale, soaking our knees as it becomes bilgewater. We eddy right at the bottom of the rapid, and the whirlpool swings our canoe against the cliff's base. New York asters cling to tiny pockets of soil in the cliff face, their electric-blue ray flowers a dramatic and shocking brightness, flower against rock.

We camp in the field at the foot of Golden Rock. Far after midnight I step from my tent into the gelid air. Frost covers the long grass, white in the starlight. The new moon is not yet up, but Golden Rock still glows faintly. Overhead a symphony of stars is scattered across the firmament in a profusion invisible in less rural places. From the other side of the river comes the distinctive five-note call of a great horned owl, a reminder that however peaceful this evening may seem for us humans, predator and prey still carry on their eternal dance of life and death.

At dawn a mist hangs over the river, dampening all sound, enveloping the shorelines in mystery. In another hour the sun will burn off the fog and mists will rise wraith-like before disappearing into the warming air, but now the air is chill and humid and still.

A loud splash disturbs my reverie. Over against the cliff, a bear is swimming, trying to find a place to get out of the water. Apparently she fell from a ledge partway up the face. She is black and not all that big and cares not a whit about us. Despite a barking dog in the campsite, she does not even deign to look in our direction. I am strangely calm. Seeing in real life the animal that has been the primary occupant of my fear closet for so many nights of camping is somehow anticlimactic. The bear gives up on trying to scramble up the rock, reverses direction, swims vigorously across the river, and bounds up the beach and into the forest. It's an impressive display of speed and strength.

As the day begins to warm and the sun illuminates the river, we launch the canoes. We have another dozen miles to go, full of lazy paddling in the unusual warmth that is more typical of late summer than fall. The water is crystal clear and every pebble on the river bottom can be clearly seen. Recent frosts have killed off all the algae that in warmer weather make the river an opaque green. The Shenandoah unwinds its miles slowly, meandering past the hogback rocks where Overall Creek comes in, the bend to the right that reveals a mile of fast-moving rock gardens, the sudden appearance of the two-foot drop of Invisible Ledge, and the narrow and twisty confines of the millrace. Finally, we emerge from that narrow valley into a pastoral landscape populated by attractive farms, and we take out at a low-water bridge.

This two-day canoe trip has been a pleasant and mostly uneventful weekend. That nothing dramatic has occurred does not bother us. After our twenty autumns of paddling trips here, the river holds few surprises. Like an old friend, it is comfortable. Memories of this trip will carry us through the long, cold winter, until lengthening days and a warming sun bring us back yet again to paddle the Shenandoah.

November

Witch Hazel in Bloom

The last flower to bloom in the calendar year is that of a small forest tree or large shrub known mostly for a medicinal extract made from its bark and leaves, witch hazel. The flowers are about an inch across with four thin, wavy yellow petals that are quite conspicuous in November, and indeed throughout the winter. One folk name for this plant is winterbloom. Witch hazel is the only plant that has flowers, fruits, and next year's buds present all at the same time. The fruit is a capsule that explosively ejects small black seeds as far as thirty feet.

Witch hazel is a small forest tree that forms flowers later in the year than any other plant in Maryland.

While the witch hazel tree is familiar to hikers, naturalists, and others who spend time in our forests, more people know the name as that of an old and inexpensive extract useful for problems of the skin. Witch hazel extract is astringent, due to its tannin content; it causes blood vessels to contract when it is applied topically. It is useful in treating insect bites, acne, hives, sunburn, diaper rash, and is a common ingredient in hemorrhoid creams.

Where to see witch hazel this week: This small tree resides in most Maryland forests but is often unrecognized until it flowers. Among the many forests that contain witch hazel are those of Gunpowder Falls State Park and the C&O Canal towpath.

Water Clarity in Chesapeake Bay

Late October and early November is often a period of settled weather in the mid-Atlantic region. Hurricanes are rare, the thunderstorms of summer are past, and those winter cold fronts sweeping down from the Arctic usually lie in the future. If winds are calm for a protracted period during these weeks, water in Chesapeake Bay can become wonderfully clear, with every shell and stone visible to ten feet down. While admittedly a rare phenomenon, these periods of extreme clarity give us a sense of what Chesapeake Bay once was like year-round, and where we hope it will return once we "save the Bay" (as the Chesapeake Bay Foundation implores us to do).

Water clarity (or the lack thereof) in Chesapeake Bay is influenced by two major factors: the concentration of microalgae and the amount of suspended sediment. Before European colonization almost four hundred years ago, algae levels were low, because their growth was limited by low natural levels of nitrogen and phosphorus. Furthermore, the algae that were present were effectively filtered from the water column by immense shoals of oysters. As the Bay watershed has been converted from forest to farmland and cities, excess fertilizer from croplands and nutrients from sewage treatment plants has fueled immense growths of algae. Similarly, development removes the filtering ability of the land, and the resultant sediment inputs to the Bay water have increased exponentially.

With the onset of cold water temperatures in late October, algae die back, so the Bay's water clears measurably by midautumn. Fall in Maryland is usually the time of year with the least rainfall, and river levels are typically at their lowest levels, so little sediment is washed into the Bay. Occasionally, these conditions conspire to produce crystal clear water in Chesapeake Bay, reminding us of what the Bay once was, and what it might be again.

Bald Cypress Leaves Turning Rusty

Among the most conspicuous trees whose foliage is now changing color is bald cypress. Bald cypress may be the most beautiful tree native to Maryland, and it is arguably the most interesting. Happiest in southern swamps, it reaches its northerly limit in and around the Pocomoke River drainage basin. Mature bald cypress trees are tall; the feathery, light green foliage towers over the rest of the forest canopy. While bald cypress is a conifer, its needles turn a brownish red in early November and then are shed, giving the tree its "bald" moniker. The bark of bald cypress is stringy and has a rich ocher color. The wood is virtually impervious to rot and so is favored for home construction. Most unusual are the many "knees," woody root projections that surround the base of every bald cypress. While they surely help with stability in mucky swamp soils, they may also play a role in respiration.

Bald cypress trees lose their needles each autumn, unlike most other cone-bearing trees. Knobby protrusions of wood at the base of most bald cypresses, called "knees," provide support.

Where to see bald cypress this week: The Pocomoke River basin has extensive stands of bald cypress; visit Pocomoke River State Park and the Snow Hill city parks. In Delaware, Trap Pond State Park also has many fine old cypress. On the western shore, there is a disjunct population at Battle Creek Cypress Swamp Sanctuary.

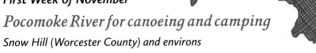

Pocomoke River for canoeing and camping

Snow Hill (Worcester County) and environs

What to see and do: Prime fall color arrives late on Maryland's lower Eastern Shore, and in early November the russet hues of bald cypress trees dominate the swamps of the Pocomoke River watershed. Late autumn is a wonderful time to camp in Maryland's excellent state parks; cool nights by a campfire and bright crisp days can make family memories for a lifetime. Two of Maryland's finest campgrounds are in Pocomoke River State Park: both the Shad Landing area and the Milburn Landing area feature large riverfront sites under tall loblolly pines. Some of Maryland's best paddling is here as well. Corkers Creek, Nassawango Creek, Dividing Creek, and the main stem of the Pocomoke are all within a dozen miles of the park. Canoe and kayak rentals are available from an outfitter in nearby Snow Hill.

Naturalist's tip: The farther upriver you paddle on tiny tributaries, the more wildlife you are likely to see. In autumn, ducks, like mallards and wood ducks, prefer remote wooded sloughs. Learning to paddle quietly will help you see more wildlife as well.

More information: On Maryland state parks, visit www.dnr.state.md.us/publiclands/. For information on canoe and kayak rentals in the Pocomoke River area, visit www.pocomokerivercanoe.com.

Whitetail Deer Rutting

Colder weather and shorter days induce the onset of breeding activity in whitetail deer: estrus in females, the rut in males. Focused on sex, whitetails move around a great deal and pay less attention to their surroundings than they do the rest of the year. This means that you are much more likely to see a deer in November than at any other time. The second week in November is probably the peak rut in central Maryland, although it begins in late October and continues until about the end of November.

Many mammals are sensitive to changes in day length, and these changes can affect reproductive hormones. Female whitetail deer respond to shortening days with increases in gonadotropic hormones that cause maturation of the ovarian follicles and secretion of estrogen. Does release pheromones that attract bucks, and they exhibit sexually receptive behaviors. They are said to be in estrus. Similarly, by early fall, male whitetails have regrown antlers, rubbed off the live tissue ("velvet") from those antlers, and become more attentive to females. With high levels of male hormones flooding their bodies, bucks seek out estrus females for mating. As in all mammals, these high hormone levels cause atypical behaviors that focus on mating, to the exclusion of virtually everything else.

For the most part, the bucks chase the does, but there is some evidence that does may leave their home range and go on "excursions" in search of a mate as they come into estrus. This is especially true in populations where the sex ratio is skewed in favor of females and in marginal habitat where bucks may not be robust specimens of ungulate manhood. So not all movement of deer during the rut is due to males chasing females.

In Maryland, the modern firearm season for deer hunting (as opposed to the bow-and-arrow and muzzleloader firearm seasons) traditionally begins the Saturday after Thanksgiving, when the rut is subsiding. This date is in a sense an anachronism of the era when whitetail deer were uncommon. With virtually all the does now bred to insure good numbers in the next year, males become superfluous and may be harvested. Hence, hunting season in Maryland is largely based upon the dates of the rut and was originally calculated to conserve the deer population.

Where to see whitetail deer this week: Whitetails are common almost everywhere in Maryland but are perhaps easiest to see where they are not hunted, or where hunting is tightly controlled. Thus, places like Loch Raven Reservoir watershed north of Baltimore City, Patapsco State Park, Rock Creek Park, and the C&O Canal towpath all have very high concentrations of deer. Dusk is the likeliest time to see them, although a nighttime stroll through neighborhoods adjacent to such parks with a flashlight in hand will also reliably yield good spottings.

Prime Fall Color on the Eastern Shore

The lower Eastern Shore of Maryland retains the warmth of summer a bit longer than elsewhere in Maryland, an effect due primarily to the moderating influence of the slowly cooling waters of the Chesapeake Bay and Atlantic Ocean. Hence, autumn comes a week or two later to this region. Prime fall color typically occurs early in the second week in November.

Where to see prime fall color this week: Parks like Tuckahoe and Pocomoke River State Parks are good choices for November fall color on the Eastern Shore.

Norway Maple Leaves

Among the many non-native plant species that have become established in Maryland, few are more conspicuous or ubiquitous than Norway maples. This moderately sized tree was brought to the American colonies by the famous botanist John Bartram in 1756, and it has since spread in cities, suburbs, and forests throughout the eastern United States. Norway maples leaf out a week or two before most other trees in our area in spring and have a somewhat darker green foliage. In autumn, while the rest of the forest trees have lost their leaves by mid-November, Norway maples still glow a brilliant yellow against the gray bare branches of the late autumn forest. Norway maples have the largest leaves of our maples; they are about as wide as they are tall and their five lobes are U-shaped (like those of the sugar maple) rather than V-shaped (like red and silver maple). The easiest way to distinguish a Norway maple from a sugar maple is to pluck off a leaf. Norway maples leak a white juice from the severed leaf stem, a trait not shared by native maples. The heavy shade cast by a Norway maple prevents the growth of most other plants, making it an ecologically undesirable species of tree.

Where to see Norway maples this week: Norway maples are common as an ornamental tree in yards and along streets across much of Maryland and have

Norway maple leaves turn yellow a few weeks later than when most other maples don their fall colors. Norways are easily identified by a white sap that drips out of the cut leaf stem.

become naturalized in many of our parks, both rural and urban. Patapsco Valley, Gunpowder Falls, Tuckahoe, and Seneca Creek State Parks all have Norway maples, as do more urban parks like Rock Creek in Washington, D.C., and Leakin in Baltimore.

TRIP OF THE WEEK
Second Week of November
The Waterfowl Festival
Easton (Talbot County)

What to see and do: On the second weekend in November, the small city of Easton, Maryland, is transformed into the waterfowl capital of the world. For more than three decades, the Waterfowl Festival has been the premier venue for wildlife art, including paintings, carvings, photography, and hunting decoys. The skill of many of the participating artists is impressive. The ducks are so realistic you fully expect the birds to get up from the display table and waddle away. With a dozen venues spread all over town and buses to transport visitors between locations and activities, the entire town is given over to every possible aspect of waterfowl conservation and hunting. Among the events not to be missed are the world championship goose calling contest and the hunting dog demonstrations. Carvers show how to create the finely detailed feathers of a songbird and painters share some of the finer points of their craft. There are plenty of activities for kids as well. A crisp fall day spent at the Waterfowl Festival is a true celebration of the human need to create art around the things we love best in the natural world.

Naturalist's tip: Only a fifteen-minute drive outside of Easton is Pickering Creek Audubon Center. With 400 acres of fields and forest and more than a mile of waterfront, Pickering Creek makes a wonderful complement to the Waterfowl Festival.

Various ducks and shorebirds frequent the man-made wetlands to the left of the entrance drive. There are even boardwalks to keep your feet dry and blinds from which to observe birds without disturbing them.

More information: For more about the Waterfowl Festival, visit www.waterfowlfestival.org. Pickering Creek information can be found at www.pickeringcreek.org.

· Week 3 ·

Ducks Arriving from the North

By mid-November, rivers and impoundments of Maryland's Eastern Shore have filled with an assortment of ducks recently arrived from Canada and the northern tier of the United States. The dabbling ducks, which include black ducks, gadwalls, northern pintails, American wigeon, and northern shovelers, prefer shallow, sheltered waters where they can feed by tipping—head down into the water and butt up above. Diving ducks, such as ring-neck, canvasback, scaup, bufflehead, and ruddy ducks obviously prefer deeper water, which are consequently more exposed waters. All of these waterfowl nest and raise young to our north during the long days of summer but must retreat to warmer climes with open water for winter. Should our winter be particularly harsh, with extensive ice, many of these ducks will move

The feather patterns of many ducks, including this northern pintail hen, are intricate and beautiful.

even farther south for the depths of winter. But while they are here, this diversity of waterfowl make it worthwhile to brave cold weather and gusty winds for a day of excellent birding.

Where to see ducks this week: Reliable locations for ducks include Eastern Neck, Blackwater, Bombay Hook, and Chincoteague National Wildlife Refuges (respectively in Kent and Dorchester Counties, Maryland; Kent County, Delaware; and Accomack County, Virginia).

Blue Crabs Preparing to Overwinter

Few animals are more beloved to Marylanders than the Chesapeake Bay blue crab. They're not cute like fawns, they're not awe-inspiring like eagles, but gastronomically, they have no equal. Whether steamed and picked over a newspaper-covered picnic table, or with their meat molded into a perfectly broiled jumbo lump crab cake, most Marylanders wax rhapsodic over the virtues of *Callinectes sapidus.*

Late autumn brings mature female blue crabs to the deep channels of the lower Bay, where they burrow in the mud and stay in a state of torpor until the water warms the following March. Many of these females are carrying masses of eggs that will hatch in the spring, renewing the species for the future. Male blue crabs also overwinter in mud, but usually more toward the less saline waters of mid-Bay.

Blue crabs are the cornerstone of the Bay's seafood industry, now that the once-plentiful quantities of oysters and many fish have been depleted; but the blue crab population declined 70 percent between 1990 and 2007. In an effort to restore blue crabs and ensure a sustainable harvest, Virginia, where the female crabs overwinter, in 2008 banned winter dredging, a harvesting method that took mostly pregnant females. In addition, both

Virginia and Maryland prohibited the harvest of female crabs at certain times and places. The results of these regulatory actions were nothing short of spectacular, and by 2011 blue crab numbers had rebounded to a level that should allow a sustainable and economically profitable harvest into the future, while ensuring enough surviving crabs to fulfill their role in the Bay's ecology.

Blue crabs have a complex life history. When an egg hatches, it gives rise to a microscopic larval stage known as the zoea. Less than a millimeter long and looking not at all like a crab, zoeae feed on plankton and grow by molting. Hatching near the mouth of the Bay, zoeae ride the tides and are swept out to the Atlantic Ocean. After as many as seven molts, zoeae move back into the Bay and transform into a quite different form, the lobster-like megalops. This free-swimming predator, only a few millimeters long, stays near the bottom of the Bay and migrates northward to less saline waters. After several weeks of life as a megalops, it molts into a juvenile stage that for the first time actually looks like a tiny crab. Young, growing crabs seek the shelter of beds of submerged aquatic vegetation. Eighteen to twenty molts and twelve to eighteen months later, blue crabs reach sexual maturity. A female mates only once in her lifetime, storing sperm for as long as a year and using it to fertilize eggs as she extrudes them onto the "apron" on her abdomen.

TRIP OF THE WEEK
Third Week of November
Bombay Hook National Wildlife Refuge
10 miles north of Dover, Delaware (Kent County)

What to see and do: Delaware may be the second-smallest state in the Union, but it boasts several wonderful natural areas within an easy drive of Maryland's population centers. During the spring and fall migrations, Bombay Hook National Wildlife

Refuge, near Dover, is a busy and enchanting place for birds and for people who enjoy seeing birds. By late November, immense flocks of snow geese have arrived from the Canadian Arctic and will spend the winter feeding in the extensive marshes of Delaware Bay and on the thousands of acres of fallow cornfields surrounding Bombay Hook. In addition to snow geese, Bombay Hook harbors the mid-Atlantic's best diversity of easily viewable ducks, whose numbers peak in November. From the twelve miles of dirt roads, one can observe most birds through an open car window without disturbing them; there are also three observation towers accessed by short walks through upland habitat.

Naturalist's tip: Parts of the refuge are sometimes closed in autumn for hunting. You'll want to check in advance and avoid those days, so that you have more habitat to enjoy on your drive through the refuge. These same roads are open to bicycle traffic. If the weather is pleasant and not too windy, cycling the refuge roads is a good choice. You'll need a mountain bike, as the roads are dirt and occasionally rocky.

More information: Visit www.fws.gov/northeast/bombayhook.

Osage Oranges Falling

What are those funny-looking, yellow-green, softball-sized fruits that accumulate in drainage ditches and are squashed on local roads at this time of year? They are the fruit of the osage orange tree. The exterior of these fruits, known to kids as "monkey brains," has many convolutions and fissures, while the interior is filled with a white sticky sap. The fruit has a faint aroma similar to that of an orange, but the species is not closely related to any citrus tree. The fruits often contain no seeds but somehow manage to form anyway. Unlike virtually every other fruit, no animals (save the occasional squirrel) eat the fruit of osage orange, so a fallen fruit often persists for quite some time.

The fruits of osage orange trees are softball-sized, with a convoluted and invaginated surface that resembles the human brain.

Osage orange trees are relatively small, no more than a few dozen feet in height, with a dense unorganized filigree of branches. Native to Texas and Oklahoma, osage orange trees were planted extensively as windbreaks during the 1930s. They are now found in all forty-eight contiguous states. The tree has large thorns but is otherwise nondescript and rarely noticed until the fruits are shed. The stripped wood is a beautiful yellow-orange and is extremely strong and limber; it is considered by some to be the equal of English yew for the construction of powerful hunting bows.

Where to see osage oranges this week: Look for this subcanopy tree in locations that were once farms or estates. The Loch

· Week 1 ·

Tundra Swans Arriving

From far up in the winter-blue sky comes the sound of waterfowl music, melodious calls that drift over the landscape, a magical sound evoking wild Arctic landscapes where humans are only occasional visitors. A skein of white birds spreads across the sky. Larger than snow geese, tundra swans are now arriving from late autumn staging grounds in the upper Mississippi valley.

Tundra swans have snow-white plumage and black feet and bills. They are slenderer, straighter of neck, and a bit smaller than the familiar mute swans of marshes and suburban ponds, which are easily identified by their orange bills. About 15,000–20,000 tundras overwinter in the Chesapeake Bay region. Historically, they fed on submerged aquatic grasses and soft clams, but they have now mostly switched to winter wheat and waste grain in agricultural fields, as water quality problems have reduced both aquatic vegetation and the number of mollusks in the Bay over the last few decades.

Tundra swans leave the Bay in early March for a staging area in the lower Susquehanna River valley. Come spring, they will follow the receding snow line, arriving on the shores of Hudson Bay or the Arctic

Tundra swans are regal and delicate in appearance, but their long-distance migration route, from the Arctic to here, implies a hardy constitution and great strength.

Ocean by mid-May. There they will breed and nest on a narrow band of wetland and tundra, thousands of miles from us and our memories of this beautiful winter guest.

Where to see tundra swans this week: Chincoteague, Blackwater, and Bombay Hook National Wildlife Refuges usually host tundra swans in winter.

Beefsteak Plant's Fragrant Flowerstalks

The onset of frost brings death and decay to most herbaceous plants, but the dried flowerstalks of one common and conspicuous herb persist throughout the winter. Strip off the gray withered flowers of the beefsteak plant, rub them between your palms, and you can enjoy a refreshing scent any time

until spring. This unusually named plant arrived in the new world from Asia and is now common and invasive.

Beefsteak plant, which stands about a foot tall, grows in disturbed soil along trails, roads, and rights-of-way in full to partial sunlight. Ovate, toothed leaves grow opposite one another on a four-sided stem. The

The dried flowerstalks of beefsteak plant exude a pleasant, minty scent when crushed.

leaves are a dark green, often tinged with purple. Small flowers grow along reddish-purple stalks that arise from leaf axils or the shoot apex. The flowers are an attractive purple color in late summer, and dry in place by late fall. Both leaves and flowers are fragrant, reminiscent of basil.

Beefsteak plant is used as both a potherb and in traditional herbal medicine in its native Asia. The fresh leaves can be added to a stir-fry with oil, ginger, and garlic. In China, the dried leaf is thought to be helpful for a wide range of ailments, and it is often mixed with other herbs. Steeped in hot water to form a tea, the leaves of beefsteak plant may ease cold symptoms. The oil that gives the plant its distinctive scent, perillaldehyde, has anti-inflammatory properties. The crushed leaves, rubbed on trousers, may deter ticks and other biting insects. Beefsteak plant gets its common name from the fact that some varieties appear so red/purple in color as to resemble a side of beef.

Where to see beefsteak plant this week: This small herb is common along trails in our parks. Check the Northern Central Railroad Trail in Gunpowder Falls State Park, the Grist Mill Trail in Patapsco Valley State Park, Sugarloaf Mountain, and the C&O Canal towpath, among many others.

TRIP OF THE WEEK
First Week of December

Bald eagles at Conowingo Dam
13 miles north of Havre de Grace (Harford County)

What to see and do: For a few weeks in November and early December, large numbers of bald eagles gather just below Conowingo Dam near Havre de Grace. Located on the Susquehanna River in the northeastern portion of Maryland, just a few miles upstream of tidal influence, this area may be the best location for viewing bald eagles east of the Mississippi River valley. From the small park at the base of the dam, eagles are continually in view, soaring over the river, and they often perch in the trees lining the parking lot. Although the eagles are clearly visible to the naked eye, binoculars are advisable for a really good look. Almost always there are friendly birders with spotting scopes who may allow you a frame-filling view of our national bird. Fortuitously, the sun is at your back all day long, affording excellent light for photography, although these days near the solstice are short. While a few bald eagles are present year-round at Conowingo, their numbers peak in late fall, in that short window between their arrival during the fall migration southward and their dispersal in late January for the beginning of the nesting season. The park at the base of the dam is private, but the dam owner, Exelon Corporation, kindly allows public access to what is formally known as Fisherman's Park at Shure's Landing.

Naturalist's tip: In addition to eagles, the waters below the dam attract a wide assortment of gulls; experienced birders know this as one of the best places in Maryland to see uncommon and vagrant species of gulls. Great blue herons nest on the island visible from Fisherman's Park and are always present.

More information: Visit www.harfordbirdclub.org/conowingo .html.

Asiatic Bittersweet Fruits and Seeds

Few fruits are showier than the red-orange arils of Asiatic bittersweet. Late autumn marks the time of year when the widespread distribution of this non-native, invasive vine becomes most evident. Asiatic bittersweet prefers lots of sunlight but is shade tolerant, and so, while it is most often found on the edge between forest and field, it can also grow in habitats as diverse as coniferous forests and the interdune zone of barrier islands.

Asiatic bittersweet grows as a perennial climbing vine that can easily smother shrubs and small trees. The flowers are inconspicuous but produce yellowish fruits that break open around first frost to reveal three bright red-orange capsules, each with two seeds. The flowers arise from many points on the stem, so each plant has hundreds of gaudy fruits. These fruits are eaten by a variety of songbirds, including mockingbirds, starlings, blue jays, and chickadees, but are poisonous to humans. The ubiquity of the discarded red portion of the fruits littering the ground gives testimony to the seeds' popularity as a winter wildlife food. Most plants have so many fruits that some seed capsules still remain at winter's end. Asiatic bittersweet was brought to the United States to grow for use in winter wreaths, for which it is an attractive addition, but then quickly

The orange and red fruits of Asiatic bittersweet brighten the winter forest and are a favorite food of many birds.

escaped cultivation, spread, and became naturalized to North America.

Asiatic bittersweet is common, but a quite similar native species, American bittersweet, also grows in Maryland. The two plants are easily distinguished: the native has leaves twice as long as wide, whereas Asiatic bittersweet has oval leaves; and the native has flowers (and thus fruits) only at the tip ends of stems. American bittersweet is becoming increasingly rare due to hybridization with and competition from Asiatic bittersweet.

Where to see Asiatic bittersweet this week: This climbing vine is extraordinarily common and quite noticeable at this time of year. Look for the orange-red capsules along sunny edges like trails and the border between forest and field. Examples of such habitat include the Grist Mill Trail in Patapsco Valley State Park and the Washington and Old Dominion Trail in the Virginia suburbs of Washington, D.C.

Christmas Fern

Winter woods lack the vibrant color of wildflowers and brilliantly plumaged songbirds, so we humans are perhaps more grateful for whatever remnant of color is present during the short days near the solstice. No plant is more widespread and common in Maryland forests, from the Appalachians to the coast's barrier islands, than Christmas fern. Its dark green, leathery fronds lend cheer in the cold season, whether the ground is covered with snow or is brown with frozen leaves. Christmas ferns are most common in shady deciduous forests, even in deep shade, probably because they conduct photosynthesis in the colder weather, when the trees are bare of leaves. They tolerate soils ranging from wet to dry, rocky to deep, rich to poor in nutrients, and are largely immune to the depredations of whitetail deer.

Christmas ferns are so named because they are still green at that holiday season. In addition, the L-shaped leaflet resembles a Christmas stocking.

Even an evergreen plant has to add new leaves, and mid-June is when Christmas fern does so. New leaves emerge as "fiddle-heads," coiled leafstalks similar in shape to the scroll at the end of the neck of a violin. Also in late spring and early summer, older leaves, a darker green in color, form spore cases (sori), clustered on the under-sides of these leaves; when the leaves are disturbed, a rain of cinnamon-brown spores results. Spores are reproductive structures that fall to the forest floor and germinate into small, inconspicuous leaflike structures called gametophytes. Only a few millimeters long, the gametophyte develops sex organs, which in turn produce eggs and sperm. Fertilization and growth yield a young version of the adult fern.

While Christmas ferns may have gotten their common name because they are green at that holiday season, they have another physical characteristic that reminds people of Christmas. Each individual leaf has a small bulge at the distal end, giving it the shape of that stocking "hung by the chimney with care." For these reasons, Christmas ferns are an easily identified member of the fern division.

Where to find Christmas ferns this week: Christmas ferns are common in most mature forests but are especially abundant at Sugarloaf Mountain, the C&O Canal towpath, and reservoir watersheds like Rocky Gorge, Prettyboy, and Loch Raven.

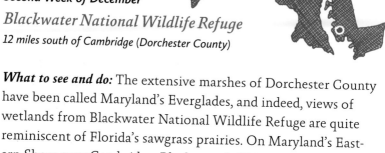

Blackwater National Wildlife Refuge

12 miles south of Cambridge (Dorchester County)

What to see and do: The extensive marshes of Dorchester County have been called Maryland's Everglades, and indeed, views of wetlands from Blackwater National Wildlife Refuge are quite reminiscent of Florida's sawgrass prairies. On Maryland's Eastern Shore near Cambridge, Blackwater's 27,000 acres are home to the largest breeding population of bald eagles north of Florida and to immense concentrations of Canada geese between November and March. While Blackwater still hosts significant numbers of ducks and other waterfowl in migration and over the winter, birding is no longer as productive there as it once was. Sea level rise, marsh subsidence, and damage by muskrats have all taken a toll on the health and acreage of the marshes. Still, Blackwater is superb year-round for bald eagles and dramatic in winter at dusk as waves of Canada geese returning to roost darken the sunset sky.

Naturalist's tip: In a bald eagle nest on the refuge, Friends of Blackwater, a nonprofit support group, has installed a camera that provides an intimate look at the domestic life and chick development of our national bird.

More information: Visit www.fws.gov/blackwater/. To view the eagle cam, go to www.friendsofblackwater.org. See also January, Week 4 in this book.

Mistletoe

How dull is a holiday party without a sprig of fresh mistletoe hung above the door? In the English tradition, anyone standing under the mistletoe is fair game for kissing. Although this particular custom goes back only to the seventeenth century, the mystical powers attributed to mistletoe are far more ancient. Druid priests used this evergreen plant as a symbol of fertility and long life. By the Middle Ages, mistletoe branches were hung above doors to ward off evil spirits and prevent the entry of witches. Extracts of mistletoe have been used in folk medicine for centuries, but science has shown them to be without beneficial effect. Mistletoe may cause gastrointestinal distress if consumed but is not as toxic as once thought.

Mistletoe, a parasitic plant, has a rootlike structure called the haustorium, which penetrates the vascular system of its host tree.

Here in Maryland, mistletoe is common on the lower Eastern Shore, growing in red maples and oaks in wetlands and along river banks. Mistletoe is hemiparasitic; its haustorium (a modified root) grows through the bark and into the xylem of its host tree, extracting water and minerals, but mistletoe also generates its own food by photosynthesis. Being evergreen, it is most conspicuous in winter, when its dull green, waxy, oval leaves stand out against the gray of bare tree branches. Mistletoe has waxy, sticky, white berries whose seeds are spread by birds.

According to tradition, mistletoe should never be allowed to touch the ground when harvested. Careful gatherers steeped in this folklore will climb the tree, attach a thin rope to the plant, then cut the woody mistletoe stem and lower the plant carefully to a waiting companion on the ground. More typically these days, however, a small caliber rifle is used to shoot twigs of mistletoe out of trees. An easier method, perhaps, but it seems disrespectful of the long tradition surrounding the harvesting of mistletoe.

Where to see mistletoe this week: Forests of the mid- to lower Eastern Shore of Maryland commonly support mistletoe, especially trees along rivers and streams. Try Pocomoke River State Park and surrounding creeks: Nassawango, Dividing, and Corkers. Note that harvesting of mistletoe is illegal in state parks and requires the landowner's permission on private lands.

Club Mosses

Another traditional plant associated with seasonal celebrations at year's end is a small group of evergreen recumbent plants of the forest floor known variously as club moss, ground pine, running pine, or lycopodium. Used to bring color to a wreath or garland of dried twigs, club mosses are actually primitive vas-

Club mosses often form a green mat across the winter-brown forest floor. This primitive plant reproduces by spores rather than by flowers and seeds.

cular plants that lack flowers and seeds. They do, however, spread via spores that are produced by specialized upright, conelike structures called stobili. The oil-rich spores of club mosses were collected by early photographers and ignited to provide a flash of supplemental light during picture taking. While club mosses are rather small and not particularly common today, they were the dominant plant on earth during the Carboniferous period more than 300 million years ago. Forests of immense club mosses up to 150 feet in height occupied much of the land then, and died and decayed to form some of what we mine as coal today.

Where to see club mosses this week: Look for club mosses on sandy soil in mature forests. Quiet Waters Park in Annapolis and watershed lands around Prettyboy Reservoir are two examples of known locations.

TRIP OF THE WEEK
Third Week of December

United States Botanic Garden
The Mall, Washington, D.C.

What to see and do: Among the museums, monuments, and official buildings of government that line the National Mall in Washington, D.C., the United States Botanic Garden is not well known but is certainly a small treasure. As the cold winds of winter sweep the Mall, this immense glass house is a warm respite for knowledgeable locals and tourists. While its floral exhibits are fascinating at any season, the holiday display, "Season's Greenings," is especially enchanting. The hundreds of poinsettias, extensive model railway garden, and other seasonal plant assemblages make the holidays a festive time to visit.

Naturalist's tip: In the last few years, the Botanic Garden has established outdoor plantings on the west side of the building. In good weather, it's an interesting stroll and a pleasant place to sit.

More information: For more detailed information, visit www .usbg.gov.

young for up to eight months post-fledging, preen each other, and associate year-round rather than just during breeding season. The roost has been described as an "information center" for black vultures; unsuccessful foragers meet there and are sometimes allowed to follow other black vultures to a carcass. Outside the extended family group, however, black vultures are aggressive and even cooperate in displacing non-kin birds.

Eventually, a few early risers test the morning's thermals, launching into the still-gelid air, soaring on six-foot wingspans, in search of warm air currents. By midmorning the roost is empty, but the skies over Talbot County are dotted with tiny specks, vultures soaring effortlessly in search of a meal.

The vultures return to their roost in late afternoon, circling and soaring for the better part of an hour before settling in. These "advertising flights" likely are meant to attract other vultures, since more birds on the roost mean more eyes alert for predators. Some of the vultures soar just above the treetops; this close look allows me to distinguish between the turkey vultures and the black vultures. While both are scavengers and are dark-colored, they are quite different in flight style and behavior. Black vultures have shorter, stubbier wings with white at the tips and a wider, shorter tail. Less aerodynamically efficient, black vultures need to flap fairly often to maintain altitude. Turkey vultures hold their wings at a shallow V angle and rock when soaring; they are also more efficient at flying and so need to flap only rarely.

As the sun sinks over Wye Island, the vultures settle into the roost. Initially a few restive vultures walk about on the ground, hopping along on mushroom-pale legs, following me as I walk down the driveway of the nature center. It makes me uneasy being followed by these birds so often associated with death. I'm eager to get to my car; vultures love to pull off windshield wipers and rubber weatherstripping, and their corrosive droppings can damage paint. As I drive away, I note a line of vultures atop the peak eave of the house, silhouetted against the evening sunset. They will sit like ebony-cowled friars through the long frigid evening, stoic and aloof, awaiting another day of soaring like dark angels, patiently waiting to clean up after death visits the animals of the winter fields and forests.

Appendix of Common and Scientific Names

American goldfinch — *Spinus tristis*
American lotus — *Nelumbo lutea*
American robin — *Turdus migratorius*
American toad — *Bufo americanus*
annual cicada — *Tibicen sp.*
Asiatic bittersweet — *Celastrus orbiculatus*
Asiatic dayflower — *Commelina communis*
Asiatic tearthumb — *Polygonum perfoliatum*

bald cypress — *Taxodium distichum*
bald eagle — *Haliaeetus leucocephalus*
beefsteak plant — *Perilla frutescens*
black bear — *Ursus americanus*
black-eyed susan — *Rudbeckia hirta*
black locust — *Robinia pseudoacacia*
blackpoll warbler — *Setophaga striata*
black vulture — *Coragyps atratus*
bloodroot — *Sanguinaria canadensis*
blueberry — *Vaccinium sp.*
blue crab — *Callinectes sapidus*
bluefish — *Pomatomus saltatrix*
broad-winged hawk — *Buteo platypterus*
brook trout — *Salvelinus fontinalis*
brown pelican — *Pelecanus occidentalis*

Canada goose — *Branta canadensis*
cardinal flower — *Lobelia cardinalis*
carpenter frog — *Rana virgatipes*
cattail — *Typha latifolia*
chestnut oak — *Quercus prinus*

chicory	*Cichorium intybus*
chimney swift	*Chaetura pelagica*
Christmas fern	*Polystichum acrostichoides*
cicada killer wasp	*Sphecius speciosus*
club moss	*Lycopodium sp.*
common milkweed	*Asclepias syriaca*
common nighthawk	*Chordeiles minor*
cownose ray	*Rhinoptera bonasus*
cranefly orchid	*Tipularia discolor*
day lily	*Hemerocallis sp.*
deer tick	*Ixodes scapularis*
diamondback terrapin	*Malaclemys terrapin*
eastern bluebird	*Sialia sialis*
enchanter's nightshade	*Circaea lutetiana*
English ivy	*Hedera helix*
false indian strawberry	*Potentilla indica*
fantail darter	*Etheostoma flabellare*
firefly	*Photinus pyralis*
flowering dogwood	*Cornus florida*
fringed gentian	*Gentianopsis crinita*
ghost crab	*Ocypode quadrata*
gray squirrel	*Sciurus carolinensis*
great blue heron	*Ardea herodias*
ground ivy	*Glechoma hederacea*
groundsel tree	*Baccharis halimifolia*
gypsy moth	*Lymantria dispar*
henbit	*Lamium amplexicaule*
hepatica	*Hepatica nobilis*
horseshoe crab	*Limulus polyphemus*

Indian grass	*Sorghastrum nutans*
jack-in-the-pulpit	*Arisaema triphyllum*
Japanese knotweed	*Fallopia japonica*
Joe Pye weed	*Eutrochium purpureum*
Lapland longspur	*Calcarius lapponicus*
large-flowered trillium	*Trillium grandiflorum*
least sandpiper	*Calidris minutilla*
least tern	*Sternula antillarum*
lesser celandine	*Ranunculus ficaria*
little bluestem	*Schizachyrium scoparium*
liverwort	*Marchantia sp.*
long-tailed salamander	*Eurycea longicauda*
lyre-leaved rock cress	*Arabis lyrata*
manatee	*Trichechus manatus*
marmorated stink bug	*Halyomorpha halys*
May apple	*Podophyllum peltatum*
May worm	*Nereis succinea*
mistletoe	*Phoradendron serotinum*
monarch butterfly	*Danaus plexippus*
morel	*Morchella sp.*
mountain laurel	*Kalmia latifolia*
mourning cloak butterfly	*Nymphalis antiopa*
mullein	*Verbascum thapsis*
multiflora rose	*Rosa multiflora*
nighthawk	*Chordeiles minor*
northern mockingbird	*Mimus polyglottos*
Norway maple	*Acer platanoides*
osage orange	*Maclura pomifera*
osprey	*Pandion haliaetus*

partridgeberry	*Mitchella repens*
pawpaw	*Asimina triloba*
Pennsylvania bittercress	*Cardamine pensylvanica*
periodical cicada	*Magicicada septendecim*
Persian speedwell	*Veronica persica*
persimmon	*Diospyros virginiana*
pinxter-flower azalea	*Rhododendron periclymenoides*
pokeweed	*Phytolacca americana*
prickly pear cactus	*Opuntia humifusa*
prothonotary warbler	*Protonotaria citrea*
purple dead nettle	*Lamium purpureum*
Queen Anne's lace	*Daucus carota*
ragweed	*Ambrosia artemisiifolia*
redbud	*Cercis canadensis*
red maple	*Acer rubrum*
red mulberry	*Morus rubra*
red-necked phalarope	*Phalaropus lobatus*
red spruce	*Picea rubens*
red-winged blackbird	*Agelaius phoeniceus*
reindeer moss	*Cladonia rangiferina*
rockfish	*Morone saxatilis*
rosebay rhododendron	*Rhododendron maximum*
sanderling	*Calidris alba*
saw-whet owl	*Aegolius acadicus*
sea nettle	*Chrysaora quinquecirrha*
self-heal	*Prunella vulgaris*
sharp-shinned hawk	*Accipiter striatus*
skunk cabbage	*Symplocarpus foetidus*
snow bunting	*Plectrophenax nivalis*
snow goose	*Chen caerulescens*
spotted wintergreen	*Chimaphila maculata*

spring beauty	*Claytonia virginica*
spring peeper	*Pseudacris crucifer*
stinging nettles	*Urtica dioica*
strawberry	*Fragaria vesca*
sugar maple	*Acer saccharum*
sweetbay magnolia	*Magnolia virginiana*
tickseed sunflower	*Bidens sp.*
trailing arbutus	*Epigaea repens*
trout lily	*Erythronium americanum*
tundra swan	*Cygnus columbianus*
turkey vulture	*Cathartes aura*
Turk's cap lily	*Lilium superbum*
Virginia bluebells	*Mertensia virginica*
white mulberry	*Morus alba*
whitetail deer	*Odocoileus virginianus*
wild cranberry	*Vaccinium sp.*
wild geranium	*Geranium maculatum*
wild rice	*Zizania aquatica*
witch hazel	*Hamamelis virginiana*
woodcock	*Scolopax minor*
wood frog	*Rana sylvatica*
yellow lady's slipper orchid	*Cypripedium calceolus*
yellow perch	*Perca flavescens*

Selected Bibliography

PRINT

Ellison, Walter G., ed. *Second Atlas of the Breeding Birds of Maryland and the District of Columbia.* Baltimore: Johns Hopkins University Press, 2010.
An invaluable reference for anyone serious about birding in Maryland.

Fleming, Cristol, Marion Blois Lobstein, and Barbara Tufty. *Finding Wildflowers in the Washington-Baltimore Area.* Baltimore: Johns Hopkins University Press, 1995.
A fine compendium of the flowering plants that grow locally, including phenology.

Lippson, Alice Jane, and Robert L. Lippson. *Life in the Chesapeake Bay,* 3rd ed. Baltimore: Johns Hopkins University Press, 2006.
Simply the best book ever published on the full diversity of animal life in the Chesapeake Bay environs.

MacKay, Bryan. *Hiking, Cycling, and Canoeing in Maryland*, 2nd ed. Baltimore: Johns Hopkins University Press, 2008.
The best places to visit for hiking, cycling, and canoeing with lots of information on the natural history of each venue.

Musselman, Lytton John, and David A. Knepper. *Plants of the Chesapeake Bay.* Baltimore: Johns Hopkins University Press, 2012.
An amply illustrated guide to plants growing in the tidal reaches of Chesapeake Bay.

Newcomb, Lawrence. *Newcomb's Wildflower Guide.* New York: Little, Brown and Company, 1977.

Uses a unique and slightly technical system to identify common vascular flora of northeast and north-central North America. Many other wildflower guidebooks are available that use sketches or photos to identify flowers by the comparison method, but few are as comprehensive as Newcomb.

Peterson, Roger Tory. *Peterson Field Guide to Birds of Eastern and Central North America,* 6th ed. New York: Houghton Mifflin, 2010.

The original guidebook to bird identification in the field is still authoritative and easy to use, although there are many fine competitors.

ONLINE

The Birds of North America Online
http://bna.birds.cornell.edu/bna/

An online reference service sponsored by the Cornell Laboratory of Ornithology that provides comprehensive, authoritative information on every species of bird breeding in North America. While the site is available only by an expensive annual subscription, the public can access BNA for free from most university libraries.

Bug of the Week
www.bugoftheweek.com

An engaging and fascinating look at many of the common and obscure insects that share our world, written by Professor Michael J. Raupp of the University of Maryland.

Macaulay Library
http://macaulaylibrary.org
The world's largest archive of scientific audio and visual recordings.

Maryland Birding
https://groups.google.com/d/forum/mdbirding
Up-to-the-minute reports of sightings of birds in Maryland.

The Natural Capital
www.thenaturalcapital.com
A regularly updated and informative website focusing on plants, animals, and scenery in and around Washington, D.C. The site includes a calendar of events, links, tweets, and blogs.

Index

This index lists places, organisms, and concepts to which significant coverage is devoted in the text. Page numbers for photographs are in italics.

Library of Congress Cataloging-in-Publication Data

MacKay, Bryan.
  A year across Maryland : a week-by-week guide to discovering nature in the Chesapeake region / Bryan MacKay.
    pages cm
  Includes bibliographical references and index.
  ISBN 978-1-4214-0939-9 (pbk. : alk. paper) — ISBN 978-1-4214-0940-5 (electronic) — ISBN 1-4214-0939-9 (pbk. : alk. paper) — ISBN 1-4214-0940-2 (electronic)
  1. Natural history—Chesapeake Bay Region (Md. and Va.)—Guidebooks.
2. Natural areas—Chesapeake Bay Region (Md. and Va.)—Guidebooks. 3. Natural resources—Chesapeake Bay (Md. and Va.)—Guidebooks. 4. Outdoor recreation—Chesapeake Bay Region (Md. and Va.)—Guidebooks. 5. Chesapeake Bay Region (Md. and Va.)—Guidebooks. 6. Chesapeake Bay Region (Md. and Va.)—Description and travel. 7. Maryland—Guidebooks. I. Title.
  QH76.5.C48M34 2013
  578.09752—dc23
                                                                    2012041894